A
Boleyn

About the Author

Josephine Wilkinson is an author and historian. She received a First from the University of Newcastle where she also read for her PhD. She is the author of *Mary Boleyn: Henry VIII's Favourite Mistress*, a two-volume biography of Richard III, the first volume of which, *Richard III the Young King To Be*, is published by Amberley. She has also edited a new edition of Paul Friedmann's *Anne Boleyn*. She lives in York.

Also by Josephine Wilkinson

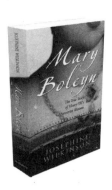  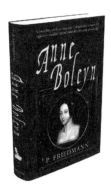

Anne Boleyn

The Young
Queen To Be

JOSEPHINE
WILKINSON

AMBERLEY

This edition first published 2011

First published in 2009 as *The Early Loves of Anne Boleyn*

Amberley Publishing
The Hill, Stroud
Gloucestershire, GL5 4EP

www.amberleybooks.com

British Library Cataloguing in Publication Data.
A catalogue record for this book is available from the British Library.

ISBN 978 1 4456 0395 7

Typesetting and Origination by Amberley Publishing.
Printed in Great Britain.

Contents

Introduction

We all know Anne Boleyn as the second wife and Queen of Henry VIII. Imagine, though, Anne Boleyn as the Countess of Ormond and Ossory; or Anne Boleyn as the Countess of Northumberland. Perhaps we might envisage Anne as the long-term mistress of an attractive and romantic poet, living out her life with him and their children in the beautiful castle of Allington in Kent.

Each of these possibilities could have become a reality for Anne before she met Henry VIII. Long before she entered the English court, while she was still learning the graces that would mark her out, her hand was the object of negotiations between her father, Thomas Boleyn, and the Anglo-Irish chieftain Piers Butler, Earl of Ormond and Ossory. Piers' son, James, was to marry Anne and take her away to his estates in Tipperary and Kilkenny.

While the negotiations for this arranged marriage were still on-going, Anne attracted the attention of the very eligible Henry Percy, heir to the earldom of Northumberland. Whatever her father, the King and Cardinal Wolsey thought of the match, Percy at least had the virtue of being in love with Anne; and, it seems, his love was returned.

Finally, Anne excited the interest of one of the most popular men of his day: the poet Thomas Wyatt. The nature of their relationship is ambiguous. On the one hand, there is some doubt whether they were romantically involved at all; on the other, there is evidence to suggest that they were, indeed, lovers and that the only question was what kind of relationship Wyatt could offer Anne.

James Butler, Henry Percy and Thomas Wyatt knew Anne Boleyn long before she met Henry VIII. She touched their lives, as they did hers. However, the attachments were not always happy. Anne's reach was as long as the shadows that fell upon the last days of her life and these men, as well as others, became entrapped in the darkness that engulfed her. Anne Boleyn, the captivating beauty, whose lengthy sojourn in France had refined her natural sparkle, wit and sophistication, influenced the lives and the destiny of many men. This is their story.

1

Growing up at Hever 1501–1513

It was early summer when Anne Boleyn came into the world.[1] The year, although uncertain, was probably 1500 or 1501.[2] Her parents, Thomas Boleyn and Elizabeth Howard, already had one daughter, Mary; in due time, they would welcome at least three sons, Henry, Thomas and George, although only George would survive to adulthood.

The Boleyn family was by no means lowly. Anne's great grandfather, Sir Geoffrey Boleyn, had taken the route followed by many younger sons as he left his rustic family home in Norfolk in the 1420s to make his fortune in the city. In the fifteenth century, no less than the present day, the streets of London were regarded by many to be paved with gold. So they were for Geoffrey, who eventually established himself as a wool and silk merchant.

Geoffrey Boleyn was highly successful in his endeavours. He accumulated great wealth, became alderman and, in 1457, was elected Lord Mayor of London. Continuing to thrive, he was soon in a position to purchase the manors of Hever in Kent from Sir Thomas Cobham and Blickling, in his native Norfolk, from Sir John Fastolf. His fortune was further enhanced when he took as his second wife, Ann Hoo, the daughter and co-heiress of Thomas, Lord Hoo.

Sir Geoffrey's eldest surviving son, William, proved to be as successful as his father when it came to making a good match. He married Margaret Butler, the second daughter and co-heiress of the Anglo-Irish chieftain, Thomas Butler, seventh Earl of Ormond. This Irish connection was to give Anne Boleyn her famous fiery temper and striking looks. It would also, in time, provide the basis for her first proposed marriage.

William Boleyn was one of eighteen men to be created a Knight of the Bath at the coronation of Richard III in July 1483. By that time, William had become the father of several children, the eldest surviving of whom was Thomas, the father of Anne. By the time of Anne's birth, then, the Boleyn family had long ago shed all traces of their mercantile past. They had advanced through a combination of hard work, loyalty to their sovereign and prestigious marriages.

Thomas Boleyn was born about 1477, probably at Blickling which, by then, had become established as his family's Norfolk seat. Following in the footsteps of his forefathers, he married well. His chosen bride was Elizabeth Howard, daughter of Thomas Howard, the future second Duke of Norfolk. Renowned for her beauty, Elizabeth was also a direct descendant of King Edward I.

The Howards, no less than the Boleyns, had served their King well. Elizabeth's grandfather, John Howard, was created the first Howard Duke of Norfolk by Richard III. Norfolk was slain beside

Richard on Bosworth Field. His title should have passed to his son, Thomas, Earl of Surrey, but the Howards' loyalty to Richard earned them the enmity of the victorious King Henry VII. Surrey was attainted, stripped of his titles and cast into the Tower.

For three years Surrey languished in gaol. Offered the chance to escape during the Earl of Lincoln's rebellion, he refused. Solitude, idleness and fear for his life had given Surrey time to think. He sensibly realized that the only way he could restore his family honour, as well as regain his titles and lands, was to pledge his allegiance to King Henry. This he did, and, in May 1489, upon his release from the Tower, Surrey's title was restored, although many of his lands remained in the hands of the King. He was sent to Yorkshire to quell rebellion, and he remained in the north as King's lieutenant, living in the beautiful castle of Sheriff Hutton, until the following year. Surrey's worth was recognized and he began a new career in royal service. His daughter, Elizabeth, married Thomas Boleyn in or about 1498, bringing her husband 'every year a child'.

In 1505, Anne's paternal grandfather, Sir William, died. His estates were divided among his sons. To Thomas Boleyn went Hever Castle in the Weald of Kent, while James Boleyn made Blickling his principal residence. Anne, at the age of about four, travelled with her family to the Garden of England. So began an association that has become almost legendary and which has endured to the present day.

For Anne and her siblings, Mary and George, life took on a new sense of excitement as they explored their beautiful new surroundings. The area might not have been entirely strange, however. It is possible that the children had visited it before, perhaps with their father.

While George, according to tradition, went to Oxford, his sisters, so close in age, were probably educated together at home. They were taught those skills deemed necessary for a lady in the period in which they lived. As such, they learned to sew and dance, to ride and hunt, and to sing and to play instruments such as the lute and the virginals. Table manners and other *politesses* were especially prized in a woman. Anne and Mary also learned to read and write. In this regard, their father, so proficient in languages, was eager for them to excel in Latin and French as much as in English.

Thomas Boleyn possessed many of the qualities Henry VIII admired in a courtier. He was sophisticated and cultured, and a man of action. Already a squire of the body, he had been made a Knight of the Bath at Henry's coronation in 1509. From then on, he climbed still higher in the royal esteem, not least for his sporting prowess. Still, there was one thing that endeared Sir Thomas to Henry more than any other: he had supported and encouraged the King as he broke free of the suffocating restrictions that had been imposed upon him by his overcautious father and his councillors.

For Henry VIII liked nothing better than war. Warfare and all its paraphernalia: weaponry, armour and chivalry, were his passion. When he was not on the battlefield he engaged in activities that were associated with it: jousting and hunting. Once again, Sir Thomas showed himself to be in tune with his master. Thomas Boleyn was an expert hawk handler and horseman; he also shone at the joust. Yet, it was Thomas's skill in languages, coupled with an aptitude for diplomacy, that made him particularly useful to King Henry. Therefore, in 1512, Henry sent him as an ambassador to the court of the Archduchess Margaret of Austria, the Regent of the Netherlands.

The object of Thomas Boleyn's mission was to negotiate with the Archduchess, the Pope, Emperor Maximilian and Ferdinand of Aragon for the formation of a holy league in support of the church and against France. Sir Thomas and his colleagues were resident at Margaret's court for about a year, although Sir Thomas was recalled briefly during this time.

The negotiations were a success in that they achieved all that the ambassadors had set out to do. For Sir Thomas, success was measured in a more personal way as well. His talents and charm, combined with an easy-going but deferential manner, had impressed Margaret as much as they had his master. For his part, Sir Thomas had seen much about Margaret and her court that he liked. In particular he saw that she had taken upon herself the responsibility of educating her nephew, Charles, and his sisters.

Margaret, Thomas noticed, also surrounded herself with *filles d'honneur*, young women from various European courts who came to the Archduchess to be 'finished'. Thomas immediately saw the advantages such an education would afford one of his daughters if he could persuade Margaret to take her. Secure in the knowledge that he had gained her confidence, he ventured to approach the Archduchess with a special request.

It is a testament to Thomas Boleyn's ability as a diplomat and courtier that Margaret gave his request serious consideration. To his delight, Margaret agreed to take on one of his daughters at her court as *fille d'honneur* and educate her. It was now for Sir Thomas to decide which daughter, Mary or Anne, would benefit the most from the opportunity. After careful consideration, his choice fell upon Anne.

It has often been said that Anne was chosen to become *fille d'honneur* to the Archduchess Margaret because she was already more accomplished than Mary, on whom such instruction as would be received in the Low Countries would be wasted. It could be, however, that Anne had experienced some difficulty in learning French to her father's satisfaction. As will be seen, by her own testimony, Anne was proficient at speaking French well, but the writing of it had so far eluded her.

Of course, there may be reasons behind Thomas Boleyn's selection of Anne of which we know nothing. Perhaps he had decided that she should marry abroad. Whatever the case, when he returned home to England, Sir Thomas was in a wonderful position to advance his youngest daughter in a way that would change her life forever.

2

The Coming of Grace:
Anne & Margaret, Archduchess
of Austria 1513–1514

The journey from Hever to Dover was a lengthy one. It took, on average, two days to travel through the countryside of Kent towards the coast. The route followed, in part, the pilgrim routes to Canterbury before continuing on a series of posts, which had been set up by King Richard III. It was laborious and not a little daunting. For Anne, as she made her way towards the coast, the journey was even more frightening because, at the age of only twelve, she was leaving England and her family for the first time.

Waiting for Anne was the Archduchess Margaret, the Regent of the Netherlands. Margaret was the daughter of the Holy Roman Emperor, Maximilian I, and his wife, Mary of Burgundy. She was only thirty-three years old, yet she had already lived a full life. At the age of three, she had been betrothed to the thirteen-year-old Dauphin, the future King Charles VIII of France. In order to educate her in French ways and prepare her for her future role as Queen of France, Margaret was given into the care of Charles's father, Louis XI, known ominously as 'the Spider King'.

King Louis died shortly after Margaret's arrival in France but, with Charles's elder sister, Anne, as regent, her prospects did not change and life continued as planned. Margaret learned to paint and draw; she became an accomplished singer, accompanying herself on the lute. Music had a very special place at court and Margaret learned to appreciate that of the Chapel Royal. Equally importantly, she leaned to dance in the elegant French style. During this time, she became fluent in the French language, which became as natural to her as her own. In her style, her culture, her outlook, Margaret became, to all intents and purposes, a great French lady. All that she had learned, all the refinements she had acquired at the court of France were to remain with her throughout her life.

Then, in 1488, an incident occurred which brought Margaret's happy world to an end. François II, Duke of Brittany died in a fall from his horse. His daughter, the eleven-year-old Anne of Brittany, suddenly became the centre of attention. France had long desired to annexe Brittany. The Breton dukes, on the other hand, had always resisted the overtures of their more powerful neighbour. Charles immediately claimed the *garde-noble* of the daughters of Brittany. This was correctly seen by Anne as an escalation of French ambitions, which once again threatened the duchy. In an attempt to thwart them, she sought to marry the widowed Emperor Maximilian and, indeed, vows were exchanged, but only by proxy. The marriage was prevented from going any further because it would have given the Habsburgs territories on two of France's borders. Meanwhile, factional infighting among the Bretons opened the way for France to invade. Anne was captured and, forced to repudiate her unconsummated marriage to Maximilian, she reluctantly agreed to marry Charles VIII instead.[1]

This left Margaret of Austria in an awkward position. With her own marriage to Charles now no longer in prospect, Charles ought to have sent her home. Instead, he attempted to marry her elsewhere in France. It was a terrible situation. Margaret was in despair. She begged to be allowed to leave, threatening to flee Paris in her nightgown if it would secure her freedom. Eventually Margaret's wish was granted and she was sent home, where her hand was once more contested by the eligible dukes and princes of Europe.

In 1497, four years after she had left France, Margaret married Juan, Prince of Asturias and Infante of Spain. As the son and heir to Ferdinand II of Aragon and Isabella I of Castile, Juan was the brother of Katherine of Aragon, who was still languishing in England, the widow of Arthur, Prince of Wales. Margaret's was to be a double wedding: her brother, Philip, known as 'the Fair' because of his fine looks, was to marry Juan's sister, Juana.

Although a most desirable match, this, too, would end unhappily for Margaret. Juan died after only six months of marriage, leaving his widow pregnant. Margaret gave birth, but her child was stillborn. She left Spain for the Netherlands shortly afterwards.

Still, Margaret was not to remain a widow for long. The following year, 1501, she married Philibert II, Duke of Savoy. Once again, however, in matters of matrimony at least, Margaret's luck eluded her. Philibert died after three years. The marriage had been childless. Margaret, with so much to offer, was once more returned to her home in the Netherlands.

Then, in 1506, Philip the Fair died at the age of twenty-eight, his promise unfulfilled. His heir was Charles of Ghent, but he was only six years old. Too young to take power into his own hands, his aunt, the Archduchess Margaret acted as regent until the boy came of age. Thus the future course of her life was set.

Margaret was an attractive woman, with red-gold hair and a milky complexion. She had been dressed in black as a child, which accentuated the beauty of her colouring still further. Now, though she wore widow's weeds, her beauty was undiminished. On two separate occasions she was offered the hand of the newly-widowed Henry VII of England in marriage. She even allowed a painter to come to her court to capture her image for him, but she refused to take negotiations a step further; Margaret was simply not interested and she turned the King down.

If Margaret could not nurture a child of her own, then she would extend her care, her learning and her love to those of others. Charles entered the nursery at her court, as did his sisters. The eldest, Eleanor, would become, in turn, queen consort to Manuel I of Portugal and then to François I of France. Another sister, Isabelle, would marry Christian II, to become queen consort of Denmark. Then there was the youngest, Marie, the future queen consort of Louis II of Hungary and Bohemia.

In addition to her nephew and nieces, Margaret took charge of the education of eighteen *filles d'honneur*, and it was in this capacity, serving Archduchess Margaret in exchange for the invaluable wisdom and polish she would gain, that Anne Boleyn entered her household.

Margaret spent most of her time at Mechelen, or Malines, in today's Belgium. It might have been from here that Margaret wrote to Sir Thomas Boleyn with news of Anne's arrival:

> I have received your letter by the Esquire Bouton, who presented to me your daughter, who was very welcome to me, and I hope to treat her in such a fashion that you will have reason to be content with it; at least be sure that until your return there need be no other intermediary between you and me than she; and I find her of such good address and so pleasing in her youthful age that I am more beholden to you for having sent her to me than you are to me.[2]

Margaret was clearly pleased with her new charge. For Anne's part, no sooner had she arrived but she was wandering through the corridors and chambers of the palace, gazing at the beautiful tapestries, learning about designs and motifs and developing, even at this early age, an appreciation of fine fabrics and colour. The palace itself would not have seemed too exotic to Anne, who would have noticed its architectural style just beginning to make a mark in England.

Margaret, whose taste was impeccable, introduced Anne into the world of art. Treasures by Bosch, van Eyck, van der Weyden, Memlinc and Fouquet were to be found in her collection. Among her court painters were Mostaert, Coninxloo, Vermeyen and Jacopo de' Barbari. Margaret would appoint Gerard Hornebolt as her *enlumineur en titre* in 1515, but it is safe to speculate that he was already an established feature at the court and, as such, came to Anne's attention. He, his son, Lucas, and daughter, Susanna, would settle in England ten years later. It is perhaps no coincidence that one of the earliest dated portraits by Lucas Hornebolt is that of Anne's brother-in-law, William Carey.

Anne also had access to Margaret's books, among them brilliantly illuminated Books of Hours. Perhaps even more importantly for Anne, Margaret had a large collection of music books. Anne was able to cultivate her tastes, which would include the works of such composers as Josquin des Prés and his pupil, Jean Mouton, but also Pierre de la Rue, Antoine Brumel and Pierrequin de Therache. In time, Anne would become an accomplished musician, famed for her singing and her skill on the lute and other instruments. Anne might even have become a pupil of Henri Bredemers, the acclaimed organist, who had been invited to Margaret's court in 1507 to teach Charles and his sisters. His most accomplished pupil, however, seems to have been Eleanor, who showed great talent at the clavichord.

Another of Anne's achievements found its naissance at Margaret's court: she learned to be a fine dancer. Dancing was considered most important for any accomplished lady, especially if she were attached to the court, because it formed the basis of other entertainments, such as pageants.

The court of Burgundy was where the art of pageantry originated and it is where it achieved its fullest flowering. Of all the themes that might be used, the perennial favourite was the interaction between men and women within the context of courtly love. This was the time of a great revival of the chivalric romances and their motifs. One favourite motif was the castle garrisoned by women and assailed by men, their costumes and legends reflecting various virtues or desirable qualities. However, courtly love, like any other 'game' had its rules and conventions which it was important not to break. As she learned all that would make her irresistible to many men, Anne also acquired, or perhaps polished, her sense of high morality.

Nevertheless, amid all the frivolity, it must not be forgotten that Sir Thomas Boleyn's primary reason for sending Anne to Archduchess Margaret was to give her the opportunity to improve her French. The lessons appear to have begun almost as soon as she arrived at the court. Anne's teacher was Semmonet, or Symmonet, a member of Margaret's household. The teaching method used with her was relatively straightforward, Semmonet would write out pieces of text for Anne to copy. Next, he would dictate to her, with Anne writing out the words in her own spelling. This is the stage she had reached when she wrote to her father the letter which has become so famous:

Sir, – I understand by your letter that you desire that I shall be a worthy woman when I come to the Court and you inform me that the Queen will take the trouble to converse with me, which rejoices me much to think of talking with a person so wise and worthy. This will make me have greater desire to continue to speak French well and also spell, especially because you have enjoined it on me, and with my own hand I inform you that I will observe it the best I can. Sir, I beg you to excuse me if my letter is badly written, for I assure you that the orthography is from my own understanding alone, while the others were only written by my hand, and Semmonet tells me the letter but waits so that I may do it myself... Written at Veure by Your very humble and very obedient daughter, Anna de Boullan.[3]

Here, Anne is writing from La Veure, known today as Terveuren, a hunting lodge set within 700 acres of parklands about ten kilometres east of Brussels, which Margaret used during the summer months. The queen spoken of by Anne is Queen Katherine, whose command of the French language was owed to the kindly attentions of the Archduchess Margaret. Clearly, Sir Thomas had held out the promise of a visit to the English court as an incentive to his daughter to learn her lessons well. Anne, anxious to please her beloved father, is clearly applying herself to her studies and is making good progress. While it is true that Anne's orthography is somewhat unorthodox and that this letter is intelligible in parts, it is important to remember that French, like English, would not acquire its 'standard' spelling until the seventeenth century.

It would not be long before Anne had an opportunity to put her French to good use. Following the triumph, if such it may be called, of the joint invasion of Guinegate by Henry VIII and

Emperor Maximilian, and the taking of the towns of Thérouanne and Tournai, Margaret travelled to Lille, where she was met by her father and King Henry. The victory, dignified by the name the 'Battle of the Spurs' because the French troops rode off so quickly, disguised the fact that they were under direct orders from King Louis XII not to fight.[4] Henry's rather hollow victory was also overshadowed by the genuine triumph of Anne's uncle, the Earl of Surrey, over the Scots, who had taken advantage of Henry's absence to launch an invasion of England. Queen Katherine proved to be a superb general, her troops meeting the Scots at Flodden field. She then sent Henry a special trophy of her victory: the bloodstained coat of the slain King James IV. Notwithstanding all this, and Henry's misfortune in having missed the sole engagement of the French campaign, there were celebrations all round.

Considering the shortage of French speakers, it is almost certain that Anne accompanied her mistress to Lille to assist with translating. Here she would have been greeted by her father, who was paid £40 for his services on the French campaign.[5] She would also have witnessed a playful flirtation, which took place between Margaret and Charles Brandon, King Henry's boon companion.[6]

Charles Brandon, Master of the Horse and the future Duke of Suffolk, was very fond of women – indeed, at the time he already had at least three wives. Now it was Margaret's turn to feel the benefit of his charm. Still buoyant from their victory, and eager to enjoy every moment, Henry and Brandon decided to indulge in a game of courtly love with Margaret. Henry urged Brandon to propose to her. This Brandon did. Kneeling at her feet, he stole a ring from the Archduchess's finger in token of their pledge. Margaret cried out, calling her suitor *voleur*. Brandon, whose understanding of French was somewhat limited, had to be told by one of Margaret's Flemish ladies-in-waiting that he had just been branded a thief. Despite Margaret's protests that the ring he had taken was too well known and would incite gossip, Brandon, very pleased with his 'conquest', refused to return the jewel. Margaret had no desire to spoil Henry's childish pleasure, so she resisted giving way to increasing feelings of annoyance. As such, she was obliged to redeem her ring with another.

Despite Margaret's caution, the little game of courtly love had not gone unnoticed and for some time rumours spread throughout the courts of Europe that Margaret had, at last, decided to abandon her widow's weeds. Margaret emphatically denied that such was the case. If Anne did not witness this flirtation, she would certainly have heard about it. Indeed, it would be played out once more for her in the not-too-distant future; then, the gentleman would be the same, but he would play with a different lady.

Anne's polished sophistication, her accomplishments and her mastery of the French language brought her to the attention of Henry's eighteen-year-old sister, Mary Tudor. Mary required French-speaking ladies to accompany her as she set out for her new life as Queen of France. Anne Boleyn was the perfect choice.

The Rival of Venus:
Anne in France 1514–1521

Aside from the joyful celebrations over the victory at the Battle of the Spurs, serious business had been conducted at Lille. A new treaty was made between King Henry and the Emperor Maximilian. Several years previously, Maximilian had negotiated a match between his son, Charles of Ghent, and Henry's sister, Mary. Charles was only three years old at the time, and Mary eight. It would take another year before the terms were finally agreed, but in 1508, the couple were formally betrothed at Richmond.

When Henry VIII inherited the throne in April 1509, he embarked upon a policy that would allow him to follow in the footsteps of one of his greatest heroes: Henry V. For Henry, like his namesake, intended to regain the former English territories in France. This ambition, and his marriage to Katherine of Aragon, had allied him to Emperor Maximilian and Katherine's father, Ferdinand of Aragon.

Now, with the alliance apparently strong, and with gains made in France, as Henry chose to see it, the time had come to perfect the union between Mary and Charles. During the discussions at

Lille, the marriage was set to be consummated at Calais no later than 15 May 1514, which was Charles's fourteenth birthday. Before it could take place, however, a serious rift occurred among the allies. Under pressure from the Pope, Henry agreed to make peace with France. One of the first things he did was order his sister to repudiate her marriage with Charles. Instead, as a seal to the new alliance with France, Mary was to marry the French King, Louis XII.

To say that Mary was unhappy with this new arrangement would be an understatement. She was eighteen years old, fresh, beautiful, desirable, a perfect Tudor rose. Louis, at the age of fifty-two, could only be described as old. Life had not been kind to him: he was unwell, inflicted as he was with several ailments, the most obvious and crippling of which was gout. Mary took solace in the expectation that Louis could not live for very much longer. As an insurance policy against further disastrous alliances, she extracted a promise from her brother that, in the event of her husband's death, which she supposed could not be too long, she could go on to marry whomever she chose. Henry, it seems, agreed. Having secured her future, Mary prepared to face the present in her new role as the French queen.

However, Mary did not speak French well. She had simply never managed to master it. As a result, she asked for ladies who knew the language to join her entourage. That she selected Mary Boleyn, Anne's elder sister, could indicate that Mary possessed the necessary linguistic skills.

Mary Tudor also asked Anne Boleyn to form part of her entourage and to serve her as a maid of honour. This truly was a fine tribute to Anne, yet, in a way, it was also a natural progression for her. She had mastered French and had cultivated those assets which made her a desirable companion to the new Queen of France. Still, it was first necessary to get her away from the Archduchess Margaret, and this was to be no easy task.

The difficulty arose from Margaret's attitude towards the new alliance, to which Mary's marriage to King Louis XII was the seal. Margaret had set her heart upon the long-planned match between the Princess Mary and Charles, representing as it did the alliance between the English court and the Habsburgs. When Mary repudiated the union, Margaret was bitterly disappointed and, at first, she simply refused to accept it.[1]

In spite of this, Sir Thomas's request for the return of his daughter would surely not have been unexpected. The realities of politics intruded into, and superseded, personal desire. Frustrated in her hopes for the future of her nephew, Margaret now had to face letting go a young lady to whom she had become attached. Sir Thomas had to muster all his diplomatic skills as he sat down to write to ask the Archduchess to release Anne.

Although Sir Thomas had written his letter on 14 August, it had probably not arrived at its destination before Margaret left for Zeeland on the 21st. When the letter was placed into her hands, however, Margaret knew she had no option but to let Anne leave.

Whatever Anne's thoughts might have been, as she left Margaret and travelled to join her new mistress, they are not recorded. Possibly they were veiled by feelings of panic and worry as she hurried across the Low Countries and into France. Certainly, Anne does not appear to have met up with her new mistress until after the latter's arrival in France. She was, therefore, spared the horrors of a treacherous Channel crossing, during which a heavy storm had scattered the Princess's ships. Mary Tudor herself had to be rescued, sea-sick and bedraggled as she was, by a gallant courtier who had braved the powerful waves to sweep her up in his arms and carry her to safety.

Quite when the Boleyn sisters were reunited is not known. It is possible, though, that Anne had arrived in time to attend Mary Tudor at her coronation in Paris on 5 November. Even now, however, a new worry emerged to cloud her happiness. Louis XII had decided to dismiss several of his new Queen's ladies. As it turned out, Mary Boleyn was kept; possibly Anne was too. The matriarchal Lady Jane Guildford was send away because she was meddling too much in the couple's private affairs. Louis had experienced similar problems with his second wife, Anne of Brittany, whose ladies had caused division and tried to rule over their mistress. It seems also that the King feared that they might have set themselves up as spies. He feared that the same pattern would be repeated with Mary's ladies, who might relate unfavourable intelligence to the King in England. Moreover, Louis, by his own admission, was sickly and did not wish, when he was 'merry with his wife, to have any strange woman with her but one that is well acquainted withal afore whom he durst be merry'.[2] In other words, Louis was intimidated by Lady Guildford's presence and this made it difficult for him to relax in her company. Louis avowed his love for his new queen, confessing, nevertheless, that, 'or he would have such a woman about her he had lever be without her'.[3]

The many complications notwithstanding, the marriage of Louis XII and Mary Tudor appears to have been quite successful. The new King and Queen remained in Paris, although it went against Louis' usual custom of spending the winter months in his château at Blois on the banks of the Loire. It was here that his previous wife, Anne of Brittany, had died and Louis was still mourning her. Indeed, so deep had been his grief at her loss that, as her grave was being prepared, he had begged them to make it large enough for two, for, as he said, 'before a year has passed, I will be with her'.[4]

As it was, Louis' new queen, the petite and pretty Mary, very soon brought him out of his mourning clothes. His advisors and physicians even warned him not to be so vigorous, nor to change his routine quite so much in case it should prove detrimental to his already delicate health. Their advice, though kindly meant, was ignored. Louis died on 1 January 1515 after only a few weeks of marriage. His melancholy prophecy had been fulfilled.

Although the French court had been exciting, with pageants, dances, hunting and the thrill of an uxorious king, the situation now became very different. For Mary and her ladies, the court of France was now a dangerous place to be. She and her maids, including the two Boleyn sisters, were in a vulnerable position. Queen Mary dressed in white, the traditional mourning for newly widowed French queens, although she refused to accept the title of *la Reine Blanche*. She was sent to the Hôtel de Cluny, where she spent the next six weeks in seclusion within a darkened room lit only by a few candles to dispel the gloom. This was a precautionary measure for, if she were pregnant, her child, if a boy, would be the next King of France.

As it was, Mary was not pregnant. Nevertheless, the crown had already passed, with indecent haste, to Louis' successor. France's adherence to the Salic Law meant that King Louis' crown would be inherited, not by his daughter, Claude, but by her husband. The new King of France, therefore, was the nineteen-year-old, François d'Angoulême, who ascended the throne as François I.

François had married Claude of Brittany the previous year, but there was no love between the two. François really did not want to marry Claude, while her silent submissiveness spoke loudly of her feelings towards the match. The wedding had been a suitably sombre affair. François' wedding gifts to his wife were not the fine jewellery, plate and magnificent dresses that were usually presented to royal brides, but a four-poster bed and a counterpane. Following the wedding feast, François went hunting with his favourites, no doubt starting married life as he meant to go on.

Claude was pretty, but lame. It is possible that she had inherited an affliction from her mother, whose legs were of uneven length, a defect she disguised by wearing shoes with heels of different heights. Unlike her mother, however, Claude was naturally retiring, and this gave her the ability to blend perfectly with her surroundings, ensuring that she was barely noticed. Of course, she made little impression on François, who was romancing a certain Madame Dishomme at the time and saw his marriage as no reason to give her up.

In the heady days that followed François' accession, Mary Boleyn became his mistress. However, it is probable that François' attraction to Mary resulted from lust rather than from any feelings of love or affection for the young woman. He quickly tired of her and passed her on to his favourites. François then turned his attention to Mary's mistress, the ex-French Queen.

Queen Mary was a valuable jewel whom François would do well to keep for as long as possible. Certainly, it was not in his best interests to send her home, for then she would take her dowry with her. It was much better, under the circumstances, to marry her off to his own advantage. There was no shortage of suitors: the Dukes of Lorraine, Savoy and Bavaria all competed for her hand, as did the Emperor Maximilian and the Prince of Portugal.

Mary, however, would have none of it. She remembered the agreement she had made with her brother just prior to her leaving for France and now she meant to marry a man of her own choosing. Although Henry and Cardinal Wolsey would resist her, Mary would press to get her way. In this, she found a most unexpected ally.

Upon learning of the death of Louis XII, an embassy led by Charles Brandon, now Duke of Suffolk, was sent to France. His brief was to congratulate François upon his accession and to discuss business, which possibly included plans for Mary's future. Suffolk's arrival, on 27 January, meant that he had to wait for François, who had gone to Reims for his coronation. Likewise, he was unable to speak with Mary, who was still closeted in her dismal room at the Hôtel de Cluny.

François and Suffolk eventually met at Noyon on 1 February, but the formal audience was not held until the following day. The meeting dealt with the usual business of conveying condolences for the late King, expressing hopes that relations between England and France would remain cordial under the new King, and thanks for the kindness François had shown to the new widow. The public audience having ended, Suffolk withdrew to his bedchamber.

However, Suffolk had not been long retired before he was summoned back into François' presence. Upon entering the royal chamber, Suffolk could not but notice that the atmosphere had changed. François told the duke that Mary had spoken to him of her fears that her brother was planning another dynastic marriage for her. Mary had then confessed to François that she was in love with Suffolk and wished to marry him.

When Suffolk at last managed to speak to Mary, she confirmed François' version of events, but her story had a darker edge. She told Suffolk that the King had declared his love for her and that he had offered to put away Queen Claude and marry Mary instead. When she refused him, he had made ungentlemanly advances towards her. Mary, her emotions fluctuating between fear for her future and the ecstasy of the love she had for Suffolk, then fell into a fit of tears. Whether or not François would have dared to attempt to take advantage of Mary, her woeful tale and pitiful lamentation tugged at the duke's heart until, in his own words:

> [T]he queen would never let me be in rest till I had granted her to be married; and so to be plain with you, I have married her heartily, and have lain with her, insomuch as far [as in] me lies that she be with child.[5]

It took Cardinal Wolsey's great powers of diplomacy to calm Henry sufficiently to allow the couple to return home to England. Still, Henry could not remain angry with his favourite sister for long.

Where was Anne while this great love story was being played out? It is possible that she had been sent home following the weeding out of Mary's attendants. Certainly, of the two Boleyn sisters, Mary alone is known for certain to have remained with the French Queen. On the other hand, there is no evidence to support any theory that Anne was dismissed. In fact, circumstances point to the opposite conclusion. Anne, as is known, remained in France, although that does not mean that she spent all her time with Queen Mary.

A strong tradition insists that Anne had gone to the village of Brie, near Paris, where she continued her education under the care of her father's friend and kinsman, du Moulin, Lord of Brie and Fontenay. According to the abbé Lebouf, the Boleyn family had originated from the Brie area and that an ancestor, Gualtier de Boleyn, had been a vassal kinsman to the Lord of Brie in 1344. Agnes Strickland,[6] as she presents this tradition, does not suggest a date for Anne's sojourn in Brie, but, if it were true, the period immediately following the death of Louis XII would have been an appropriate time.

The tradition which places Anne in the village of Brie also appears to have been known to Nicholas Sander. According to his account which, nevertheless, is consistent with his ill-treatment of Anne's memory, Anne had been sent away at the age of fifteen at Henry VIII's own expense because she had sinned with her father's butler and then with his chaplain.

Sander's tale is untrue, but the connection with Brie might have some foundation in fact. In the end, however, the truth or otherwise of Anne having spent time there cannot really be known. So much of her life at this stage is undocumented. What is certain is that she did not return to England with her sister and Mary Tudor. Instead, she went into the service of the new Queen of France.

Queen Claude, who was only fifteen years old, was the daughter of the late Louis XII and his second consort, Anne of Brittany. She was a young woman of warm character and fine virtue. She insisted upon high morality and restraint, and showed a strict regard for etiquette. Her court was run almost as a convent, with her ladies following behind her in procession as she went about her religious observances. They accompanied her to every public appearance, models of decorum and modesty. Claude also supervised the activities of her ladies, needlework being a speciality, as well as guiding their thoughts towards holy and virtuous matters. If Claude followed her mother's example, Anne and the other maids of honour would sit on the floor, protected from the cold of the tiles only by their heavy skirts and cushions.[7]

King François spent much of his time at Amboise, where he was soon to embark upon extensive building works. Claude felt ill at ease at her husband's more exuberant court, where she was forced to suffer the indignity of a neglected wife. François gave his love to one mistress after another in a series of affairs that ranged from the very brief, as with Mary Boleyn, to the more lengthy, as in the case of Françoise de Foix, Duchess of Chateaubriand. Claude preferred to spend her time at Blois, in the pretty château perched high above the magnificent Loire valley, where she had spent much of her childhood.

Even so, Queen Claude accepted that there would be times when she would be expected to join François. Such occasions could not have been infrequent for, despite the mutual dislike that existed between her and the King, Claude was almost constantly pregnant. From the time of her marriage in 1514 to her death ten years later, she would produce seven children, although not all of them would survive infancy.

While Claude probably never entirely cast aside her proverbial wimple, she nevertheless indulged her ladies at the various entertainments laid on at François' court. Anne, in her element, let down her glorious hair and threw herself into the amusements with a passion.

A description of Anne at this point in her life by the Viscount de Chateaubriand[8] asserts her great talent for poetry and her fine singing voice. In dancing she was graceful and agile, inventing many new figures and steps which subsequently became known by her name or that of the handsome man who had partnered her. She was skilled at all the games played at court and was expert at the lute and the rebec. In matters of dress her tastes were said to have been adopted by other ladies, although, we are assured, none looked so well as Anne, who was described as the rival of Venus. Strickland offers a description of Anne's costume:

> She had a bourrelet or cape of blue velvet trimmed with points; at the end of each hung a little bell of gold. She wore a vest of blue velvet starred with silver, and a surcoat of watered silk lined with miniver, with large hanging sleeves which hid her hands from the curiosity of the courtiers; her little feet were covered with blue velvet brodequins, the insteps were adorned each with a diamond star. On her head she wore a golden coloured aureole of some kind of plaited gauze, and her hair fell in ringlets.[9]

As Strickland correctly remarks, this is not Anne Boleyn as we usually picture her, with ringlets in her hair, bells on her cape and large hanging sleeves. The description offered here would seem to refer to a dress designed and worn for a specific occasion, perhaps the costume of some character Anne was portraying in a pageant. Of course, it is not impossible that Anne experimented as much with outfits and hair styles as she did with dance-steps.

Anne's lively contribution to the entertainments of the court led to accusations against her virtue, suggesting that she indulged in the scandals for which the court of King François was so famous. This, however, stems from Sander, who lost no opportunity to malign Anne. Moreover, as is now well known, it was not Anne, but her sister, Mary, who became a casualty of François' exploitation of the ladies of his predecessor's court. It is possible, as Strickland points out, that Anne simply fell victim to the lot of all women who aspire to the leadership of the *beau monde*, who attract undesired notoriety and are thus regarded as *blasé*. Certainly, when seen in contrast with the sober and sombre court of Queen Claude, Anne could indeed be viewed in this way.

Still, life at François' court was not all frivolity, hunting and dancing. The King of France was a true Renaissance prince. He was the first prominent patron of Italian artists of his time. Among his collection was *La Belle Jardinier* by Raphael, François' portrait had been painted by Titian, while perhaps the most famous work of art belonging to François was the *Mona Lisa*. François had invited Leonardo da Vinci to France, housing him at Le Clos-Lucé in the Loire valley, where he lived out the remaining years of his life. Whether or not Anne met da Vinci can only be speculated; what can be said with certainty is that her education had not come to an end when she left the court of the Archduchess Margaret.

Moreover, there was every opportunity to put what she had learned to good use. Her dancing, her deportment and her conversation, which was already beginning to show the sparkle and wit for which she would be so famous, were all put on display when she accompanied her mistress to the meeting of the two Kings at the Field of Cloth of Gold in June 1520.

In fact, Anne's name is not mentioned among those who attended this spectacular event, but it would be difficult to imagine her not being there. First of all, her position as maid of honour to Queen Claude, who was six months pregnant at the time, would seem to ensure it. Secondly, her skill at French would certainly be needed to help with the inevitable translations that would be necessary to smooth the conversation between ladies and gentlemen of either country. Thirdly, her parents, her sister, Mary, and Mary's new husband, William Carey, and possibly her brother, George, all attended, as did their Howard relatives.

For someone of Anne's high-spirited nature, life at the court of Queen Claude might have seemed very dull. Nevertheless, when she became queen, Anne also demanded the strictest moral standards of her ladies and other servants. She would encourage them to read the Bible, even leaving an English copy open at all times in her rooms for anyone to look at as they pleased. In contrast, and here we see Margaret's contribution, her court would also be a place of dancing and music, bright and fashionable dresses, laughter and song. It seems that each of these qualities: deep and genuine piety and lively exuberance, existed quite harmoniously within Anne's own character, allowing her to thrive whatever occasion or humour demanded.

Anne's youth and early womanhood were guided and influenced by two strong women and one weak one. The first of these was the formidable Margaret of Austria. The Archduchess had been a kind mistress and a gifted teacher. Anne had learned much from her. On a practical level, under Margaret's guidance, Anne had learned to speak and write the French language, which had been the primary reason for her going to the Low Countries. In addition, however, she had learned to enjoy pageantry, where she could show off her fine singing voice and her expertise at the dance. At Margaret's court, Anne had acquired an appreciation of art and had shown an interest in architecture. Given access to Margaret's fine library, Anne was able to lose herself within the beauty of the exquisitely illuminated treasures and to further cultivate her understanding and appreciation of the French language.

Margaret had also taught Anne the art of flirtation, to accept and manage the playful – and the not-so-playful – attentions of men. From Margaret, Anne had learned that a woman could be assertive, that she could, to a large extent, be the mistress of her own destiny, to hold out for what she wanted and never to give in.

It was a valuable lesson to have mastered, one she would make use of in the years to come.

Mary Tudor had taught Anne a similar lesson. A woman could get her own way, certainly, and that she could use her wiles, even her tears, to achieve her ambition. Mary, although young, had already acquired the cunning she needed to assert herself in life and to ensure that she would not always be a leaf blown by turbulent political winds. Just setting out on life's journey, Mary, nevertheless, knew enough to secure her brother's assurance that, while she would acquiesce to his wishes on this occasion, she would not do so again. Henry had agreed, whether he meant it or not. Then, when her marriage came to its inevitable conclusion, Mary held her brother to his promise and, manipulating the emotions and the fears of the Duke of Suffolk, she achieved her aim.

Perhaps it would not be wrong to add another Mary to the list of Anne's tutors, since she proved to be a valuable teacher to Anne also. This was her own sister, although it was doubtful that Mary had Anne's education in mind as she succumbed to the charms of the flirtatious King François. Mary's experience as François' mistress, if such a brief liaison could allow her to be regarded as such, and her subsequent treatment as she was passed from one licentious courtier to another, must have shocked, and possibly even frightened Anne. While Anne had been taught about such worldly ways by Margaret, it was probably only at this point, when she discovered how women really could be exploited and mistreated, that she decided to protect her greatest asset, her purity, at all costs. Anne, at that point, vowed that she would not follow the route taken by her sister.

Anne's next tutor, Claude, Queen of France, lived in the shadows of all who came into her sphere. Claude was treated as the royal baby-maker, while King François entertained himself with a series of powerful and enchanting mistresses. From Claude, Anne could take the knowledge of the comfort and satisfaction that was to be gained by leading a life of modesty and devotion. On the other hand, she also came to see that, as her time spent at Margaret's court had shown, such virtues were not incompatible with the more extrovert activities of court dances, hunting and festivities. There was room for both styles of living as long as etiquette and moderation were observed.

Anne knew that the life of an unwanted and unloved wife was not for her. When she married she wanted a man who would love her, and who would regard her as more than merely the means of begetting heirs. Anne, after all, was now a very learned woman of polished sophistication, companionable and endowed with a natural tendency to leadership that would mark her out at any gathering. She was highly desirable; any man would be lucky to have her but, for Anne to accept him, he would have to be a special man, one whom she could love and respect, and perhaps, manage. It remained to see whether such a man lay in her destiny.

4

An Irish Alliance:
Anne & James Butler 1521–1522

'No woman has ever had such charm, such pleasing qualities
of person and character, as Anne Boleyn. I have heard that her
face had an animated, individual quality, and that she bore no
resemblance to any other English beauty.'

'I also seem to remember hearing', rejoined Mme de Clèves,
'that she was born in France.'[1]

Anne Boleyn had become so accomplished in all things French
that she was considered by some to be a Frenchwoman. However,
for all her French sophistication, Anne's roots and her destiny lay,
not in the fairytale châteaux along the Loire, but in England.

To his great dismay, King François was asked to release Anne
back into the care of her family. Shortly after she had made her
way across the stormy waters of the English Channel in late
December 1521, François wrote to his ambassadors, La Batie and
Poillot, expressing his concerns about relations with his 'good
brother', Henry VIII. Notwithstanding the promises made and
sealed at the Field of Cloth of Gold, the fragile peace between
England and France was breaking down. English scholars at the

Sorbonne were leaving for home, as was 'the daughter of Mr. Boullan'. That Anne, who was still in the service of Queen Claude at the time, had been recalled was seen as a sign of escalating hostilities between the two countries. Moreover, if more proof were needed, François noted that ships were being commissioned at Dover, musters were being taken in England and the rumour was that Henry intended to declare war on France.[2]

Whatever King François' suspicions about the reasons for Anne Boleyn's return to England, the real explanation was less sinister. For some time now, Anne had been the subject of negotiations undertaken by King Henry, Cardinal Wolsey, the Earl of Surrey and Sir Thomas Boleyn, with Sir Thomas's cousin, the Anglo-Irish chieftain, Sir Piers Butler. The object of their negotiations was to attempt to settle a dispute that had arisen between Thomas Boleyn and Piers Butler over the earldom of Ormond.

The immediate problem had begun six years previously with the death of Sir Thomas's grandfather, Thomas Butler, the seventh Earl of Ormond, in 1515. However, this was just the latest incident in a quarrel that had gone on for much longer than that. Ormond had inherited the earldom from his brother, Sir John, in 1476. Both brothers had been absent from Ireland for long periods during the Wars of the Roses and the estates had been managed by their cousin, Sir James Butler. So involved was James in the day to day running of the Ormond estates that he had come to regard them as his own property. Moreover, when the seventh earl died, James's son, Piers, considered himself to be the rightful heir.

On the surface of it, Piers Butler had a good claim. He was cousin to the late earl and he was indeed his heir male. Still more importantly, he had the backing of others among the Irish lords as well as the majority of the people. In spite of this, his claim was flawed. The earldom of Ormond was, in fact, entailed to heirs general, not specifically to heirs male. This meant that the rightful inheritors of the Ormond estates were the seventh earl's daughters, Margaret Boleyn and Anne St Leger. Margaret was the mother of Sir Thomas Boleyn, who advanced his mother's claim. King Henry, who saw in Sir Thomas a loyal and respected courtier who had already provided substantial service, was happy to grant livery of the estates to him.

Sir Piers was not happy with this decision and he continued to agitate for what he saw were his rights. He seized the late earl's estates and showed every sign that he would never relinquish his hold on them. A solution had to be found, but it had to be a diplomatic solution, as far as such a thing was possible. Sir Piers was deemed useful to the English government in its struggle to control the various Irish factions. On the other hand, the stalemate had to be broken, and the Earl of Surrey thought he had found a way.

Thomas Howard, Earl of Surrey had been sent to Ireland in the spring of 1520 as lord lieutenant. Almost from the moment he took up his post he had been assisted by Sir Piers Butler and the two men appear to have struck up a firm and genuine friendship. Nevertheless, Surrey hated his office and longed to return to England. The solution he came up with would not only solve the dispute over the earldom of Ormond to the satisfaction of all involved, it would also allow him to return home. It was quite straightforward. Sir Piers' son, James, would be married to Thomas Boleyn's daughter, Anne. The earldom of Ormond would go to Piers Butler, from whom James and Anne would inherit in due course. That way Sir Piers would formally acquire the estates and title he had long regarded as his own, while the Boleyns would see their heritage remain within the family.

Simple but effective, Surrey's plan won the approval of King Henry, who ordered Surrey to discover Butler's views about it. The following month, October 1520, Surrey and the Council of Ireland were able to assure Henry that all were agreed that the marriage would be advantageous. Wolsey, too, liked the idea, and he and the King set about persuading Sir Thomas Boleyn to agree to the plan. However, there was a problem. The primary obstacle, from Sir Thomas's point of view, was that he wanted the title of Earl of Ormond for himself. Surrey's plan, if it went ahead, would see it slip beyond his grasp. The negotiations continued.

Anne, far away in France, would not have been consulted about the proposal. It is not even certain that she would have been aware of the discussions that were taking place and that would have such profound consequences for her future. As to the prospective groom, James Butler, he might have been aware of what was being planned for him; he was certainly at the English court by this time.

Born in, or shortly after, 1496, James Butler was in his early twenties at the time his marriage to Anne Boleyn was being considered. He had spent much of his early life on the Ormond estates, which were spread across the counties of Kilkenny and Tipperary. He had made his court debut in 1513, when he joined Henry's forces for the invasion of France. Taking part in the siege of Thérouanne, he received a serious leg wound, which caused him to limp for the rest of his life and earned him the epithet, *Bocach*, 'the lame'.

Returning to Ireland, he is next encountered in March 1518 when, shortly after attaining his majority, he and his father were granted possession of the manor of Templemore. James would spend the next two years in Ireland. Working alongside his father, he learned estate management and undertook military training. This, then, was his position when the Earl of Surrey crossed over to Ireland.

With the negotiations for James Butler's marriage to Anne Boleyn underway, James was sent to the English court. It is often believed that Wolsey soon saw the young man's worth as a means of influencing events in Ireland. James, therefore, was taken into Wolsey's household to further his education, but perhaps also to act as an unwitting hostage to his father's good behaviour. In the interim, the haggling over the Butler-Boleyn alliance rumbled on.

Anne, meanwhile, had been recalled from France, possibly arriving at home in time for the Christmas festivities of 1521. It is not known whether or not she met James. Since her father quickly found a post for her at court in the service of Queen Katherine, as well as a place in the royal wardrobe, it is entirely possible that the two young people did meet. Wolsey was, naturally, frequently at court, as were the young men of his household, who formed part of his entourage.

Certainly James would stand out. A portrait once believed to be that of Thomas Boleyn has successfully been demonstrated to be that of James Butler.[3] Although it post-dates the period in which these events took place, we can still get an idea of the man Anne would have known.

James's portrait shows a powerfully-built man with a broad, open face, rosy cheeks and a pleasant expression. The portrait is little more than a drawing, but the parts that had been coloured show that James had inherited the red hair of his father. He wears a black doublet slashed to reveal the white shirt beneath, while the ensemble is finished with a bright red hat. His is a kind face, and it seems that James was hard-working, intelligent and responsible, someone Anne could certainly respect.

This, then, is the man Anne Boleyn was destined to marry. As she waited for her father and Piers Butler to conclude their negotiations, Anne threw herself into the pleasures of court life. One of her tasks as a member of the royal wardrobe was to look after the costumes that were used in the many pageants that made life at King Henry's court so interesting and exciting. As a member of that court, she donned one of the pretty dresses as she and the other young beauties took part in the Shrovetide festivities of 1522.

The Shrovetide of 1522 was given over to the theme of unrequited love. It was to be a doubly special occasion for the Boleyns. In the first place it marked the dawning of the lengthy relationship between Anne's sister, Mary, and King Henry. Still, however passionate it might have been, their affair was conducted in absolute secrecy. Few outside Mary's immediate family were aware of it, and it would remain that way until the necessity arose for Henry to admit to it. Although it was a very special occasion for Mary and her family, they were compelled to be discreet. It was just as well, then, that their excitement and exhilaration at having the King in their midst could find another outlet. Bubbling over with pride and happiness, the Boleyns delighted in their second daughter as she took her part in the festivities. For this particular Shrovetide marked the court debut of Anne Boleyn.

It was a charming scene, but not an unfamiliar one to Anne, where such occasions were a regular feature at the Archduchess Margaret's court. Wolsey's palace of York Place at Westminster had been selected for the venue. A castle of green, the *Château Vert*, had been built in the main chamber. Eight gorgeously apparelled maidens were held captive. These were the virtues or desirable qualities of the chivalric romances that went back into the mists of time. Their names were Beauty, who was played by Mary, formerly the Queen of France and now Duchess of Suffolk; Honour was played by Gertrude Courtney, Countess of Devon. Anne Boleyn appeared as Perseverance, while her sister, Mary, was Kindness. Constancy was played by the young lady who would one day be their sister-in-law, Jane Parker. Bounty was portrayed by a Mistress Brown, while a Mistress Dannet played Mercy. The eighth virtue, Pity, was played by a lady whose name is not given. The virtues wore costumes of white silk set off by head-dresses of Milan bonnets and cauls decorated with gold and jewels. They were guarded by the vices or undesirable qualities, eight 'women of India', played by boys from the Chapel Royal. These bore the names of Danger, Disdain, Jealousy, Malebouche, Scorn, Strangeness and Unkindness. The name of the eighth vice is, unfortunately, lost.

The vices guarded their captives well, but they were no match for the Lords. Dressed in eye-catching costumes of cloth of gold and mantle cloaks of blue satin, the Lords were Amorous, Attendance, Gentleness, Liberty, Loyalty, Nobleness, Pleasure and Youth. One of them was played by Henry VIII who, like the others, was disguised by a mask. The guests and onlookers feigned surprise when, once the Lords had rescued the virtues and the dancing was finished, everyone removed their masks to reveal their faces.

Each of the virtues was identified by her name, or 'reason', sewn onto her costume. It is thought that the names matched a quality or personal trait of the bearer. Why Mary Boleyn should be Kindness is self-evident, since she was the royal mistress by this time. Perhaps her 'reason' was a private joke between her and the King. Why Anne should be Perseverance is less clear. The explanation is, perhaps, hinted at in the letter she sent to her father shortly after her arrival at Margaret's court. In it, she had assured him that she was all the keener to persevere in speaking French well. Anne, it is clear, did not give up easily. Once she had made up her mind to something she would stick with it whatever obstacles might be placed in her way. She had a tenacity and strength of character that allowed her to face any challenge, take any risk.

One aspect of Anne's character, then, was displayed on her costume for all to see. Elsewhere, however, she is described as being 'full of pride, ambition, envy, and impurity'.[4] The man who described her in this way was Nicholas Sander, a recusant Catholic living in exile from his native England. At the time he made this assessment of Anne, England was ruled by her daughter, Elizabeth.

On the other hand, Anne was said by George Wyatt, the grandson of the poet, to be possessed of 'the graces of nature graced by gracious education'.[5] To Sander she was 'the model and the mirror of those who were at court', adding that she was always 'well dressed, and every day made some changes in the fashion of her garments'.[6] Of course, he was describing Anne the Queen, whom every woman would wish to emulate.

Anne's appearance, not unnaturally, inspired much debate. There are conflicting views, even when it is the same author speaking. Anne was said to be 'rather tall of stature',[7] or 'of middling stature'.[8] Sander speaks of her as having 'long black hair, and an oval face of a sallow complexion'.[9] That she was dark was also the opinion, apparently, of no less an authority than King François I, who is supposed to have said: 'Venus was blonde, it has been said: We see indeed that she is brunette.'

To the poet, Thomas Wyatt, Anne was the 'Brunet, that set my wealth in such a roar'.[10] His grandson, George Wyatt, would describe her as being 'not so whitely as clear and fresh'.[11] The Venetian ambassador, Sanuto, agreed that Anne's complexion was swarthy. He also described her long neck, wide mouth and 'bosom not too much raised'; he praised her eyes, which were 'black and beautiful'. In spite of this, he thought that Anne was 'not one of the handsomest women in the world'.[12]

When it came to Anne's beauty, there were those who would beg to differ with Sanuto. She was described by various people as 'very beautiful',[13] or 'beautiful and with an elegant figure'.[14] However, in comparison with Elizabeth Blount, formerly King Henry's mistress, Anne did not fare so well. Elizabeth Blount was said to have been the prettier of the two, but that Anne was 'the more eloquent and graceful, more really handsome'.[15] Even Sander allowed that Anne was 'handsome to look at, with a pretty mouth'.[16]

Nevertheless, Anne was said to have had some imperfections. Her most ardent detractor, Sander, speaks of a 'projecting tooth under the upper lip', which clearly conflicts with his assertion that she had a pretty mouth. He adds that she had six fingers on her right hand and a large wen under her chin.[17]

While Sander is the only source for the projecting tooth, the suggestion that Anne had a wen, or at least some other type of swelling under her chin is not unique to him. An anonymous account of Anne's coronation noted that she wore a mantle with a 'high ruff of gold thread and pearls, which concealed a swelling she has, resembling a goître'.[18] The author of this description had clearly never attended an English coronation and, as such, was unaware that coronation robes closed high under the chin. Anne, therefore, was merely wearing ceremonial dress that was appropriate for the occasion, not attempting to hide an imperfection.

Regarding her alleged sixth finger, once again, there is support for some disfigurement to one of her hands. Indeed, this might have been hinted at in Chateaubriand's description of her long-sleeved dress, which hid her hands. George Wyatt notes that 'there was found indeed, upon the side of her nail upon one of her fingers, some show of a nail'.[19] He adds that this was easily covered by the tip of one of her other fingers.

Wyatt's description hardly suggests a sixth finger. Moreover, Anne was an accomplished musician, skilfully playing the lute, the virginals and the rebec. It is difficult to imagine her acquiring such proficiency if she had an extra finger, which surely must have impeded her progress. Similarly, Wyatt makes no mention of a wen or a goitre-like swelling under Anne's chin; he says only that she had, on some parts of her body, 'certain small moles incident to the clearest of complexions'.[20]

Not unexpectedly, none of these alleged disfigurements feature in any of the extant portraits of Anne. While none are contemporary, at least some of them are probably copies or adaptations of earlier portraits, some of which might have been contemporary to Anne. Moreover, they do agree with the general descriptions of Anne's looks. Her eyes are generally shown to be almond shaped and hazel brown. Her hair, said to have been her finest feature, is dark auburn, its beauty shown off by a pretty French hood, rather than being hidden beneath the heavier English gabled headdress. Her complexion is sallow, while her fingers, where they are shown, are long and elegant. There is no trace of an extra finger, or even the small show of a nail as noted by George Wyatt.

In all, then, Anne's appearance may be summed up like this: she had hazel eyes, long auburn hair and a sallow complexion. She was possibly slightly taller than average and slim; willow-like and graceful with an elegant swan-neck. She was not beautiful in the conventional sense. Her colouring did not match the perfect English rose complexion and blue eyes so favoured at the time. However, her skin was clear and fresh, while a few moles acted as beauty spots.

However, Anne Boleyn had qualities other than her looks working in her favour. Her time in France had lent her a refinement that set her apart from the ladies at the English court. She had an inner beauty that caught the attention of men and held them in fascination. She was exotic, cultured, with a quick and clever wit; she was intelligent and intellectual, she could hold her own in conversation and, most noticeably, she was tremendously sexy.

Anne's sexiness could work either for or against her, arousing desire in some men and hostility in others. While Sander was hostile to Anne, he had not known her. Of the men who did, arguably the one who was most hostile to her was the imperial ambassador, Eustache Chapuys. He lost no opportunity to disparage Anne, yet, although he refused to speak to her or even to acknowledge her, he was clearly obsessed by her. His dispatches to his master, the Emperor Charles V, are filled with anecdotes and gossip about 'the Lady', 'the Lady Anne', 'the Concubine', 'the whore'. Yet he continued to watch her every move and seek out news of her.

Still, Chapuys belonged to a later time in Anne's life. He did not know her in the early days when she had just returned from France and was beginning to cast her spell over the entire court. During this happy time the negotiations for Anne's marriage to James Butler were still ongoing, yet her attention had already been diverted elsewhere. A young man in the entourage of Cardinal Wolsey had paid court to her and Anne, far from demurely holding him at arms length, had responded to his overtures with enthusiasm.

An Innocent Love Affair:
Anne & Henry Percy 1522–1524

Not long after she had made her sparkling debut at the pageant of the *Château Vert* in March 1522, Anne Boleyn caught the attention of one of the most eligible bachelors in the land.

Henry Algernon Percy was born about the year 1502, making him a year or two younger than Anne. His father, after whom he was named, was the fifth Earl of Northumberland, sometimes known as Henry the Magnificent. His mother was Katherine Spencer, daughter of Sir Robert Spencer, a nephew of Edmund, sixth Duke of Somerset. Through his mother, then, Lord Percy was of royal blood, being a descendant of Edward III through John of Gaunt.

The Percys were one of the greatest magnate families of the North Country. Here, with their vast estates in Northumberland, Yorkshire and elsewhere, they lived in rivalry, and occasionally in harmony, with their neighbours, the equally mighty Nevill family. By the time the Wars of the Roses had drawn to a close, however, the Percys had lost much of their influence so that many of the posts that would traditionally have gone to a Percy were instead administered by others deemed more trustworthy. One example of this migration of power was when Anne Boleyn's uncle, the

Earl of Surrey, acted as lieutenant to Prince Arthur in the council in the north.

Although the Earl of Northumberland had been made warden-general of the marches towards Scotland, it was only a ceremonial post, allowing him to escort King Henry's sister, Margaret, to her new life as Scotland's Queen. Northumberland never held office on the marches again, the post of warden-general being filled by Thomas, second Baron Dacre.

Seeing his once proud family reduced to little more than mere ornaments to be brought out on special occasions, Northumberland sought to restore Percy influence in the north. He managed only to earn the further distrust of the King. As such, the earl's son, Henry Percy, soon found himself in a similar position to that of James Butler. He entered the household of Cardinal Wolsey, where he would complete his courtly education by acting as a servant to the cardinal. However, he, like James Butler, was also a hostage for the good behaviour of his father.

Cardinal Wolsey had little love or respect for his young ward. This is usually attributed to Percy's financial ineptitude, even though he would not acquire this reputation until later in his life. Even after Percy had married and become the sixth Earl of Northumberland, the cardinal made it his business to interfere in the affairs of his former servant, treating him with the contempt he still thought he deserved. Wolsey's attitude appears to have been less to do with the young man's capabilities and more the result of a personality clash that caused so much bad blood between the page and his master.

In about the year 1516, when Henry Percy was in his fourteenth year, Northumberland opened negotiations with George Talbot, fourth Earl of Shrewsbury. The object was the marriage of the younger Percy to Shrewsbury's daughter, Mary Talbot. The match promised to be a good one. Both families were ancient and wealthy, their vast estates bordered onto each other and Mary would bring a dowry of 2,500 marks (£1,666 13s 4d) to the marriage.[1]

However, in spite of the obvious advantages, the two earls vacillated. For the next eight years, correspondence passed back and forth and, at times, the terms for the marriage seemed to have been agreed. Yet, when asked what progress had been made, Northumberland was noncommittal, answering merely that he had concluded with Shrewsbury.[2] Then, when enquirers wanted to know when young Percy might come to court, his father, with no small amount of irritation, answered: 'When he is better learned and well acquainted with his wife, shortly after that he shall come to Court.'

Yet nothing happened. Henry Percy had become acquainted with Mary Talbot and it was hatred at first sight for both of them. This, however, would have made no difference to the marriage arrangements. If their respective fathers wanted them to marry, then marry they would. Unless, that is, something occurred to put a stop to it. Whatever happened, in this case, the proposed marriage was cancelled and Percy came to court where, as noted, he became a page to Cardinal Wolsey.

At some stage young Percy's attention was caught be a scintillating young woman of charming wit, sexy eyes and coquettish demeanour, who had just returned to the English court after a lengthy stay in France. Within a very short space of time, Henry Percy was head-over-heels in love with Anne Boleyn.

Perhaps the best source for the affair between Anne Boleyn and Henry Percy is George Cavendish, although some of his statements require qualification. Cavendish[3] had entered Wolsey's household as gentleman usher at roughly the same time as the events of which he writes took place. He quickly became close to the cardinal and would remain loyal to him even after his fall. Following Wolsey's death in 1530, Cavendish was offered a place in the service of King Henry; he declined, preferring instead to retire to his home in Suffolk.

In his later years, Cavendish wrote a biography of Cardinal Wolsey which he finished, by his own testimony, on 24 June 1558. This work might have been intended as a polemic to the unsympathetic representation of Wolsey given by Edward Hall, whose *Chronicle* had appeared some ten years previously.

In his biography, Cavendish[4] tells of how Henry Percy would accompany Cardinal Wolsey on his visits to court. While his master took care of business, Percy would wander off to the Queen's chambers, where he would amuse himself in the gentle company of her ladies as he waited for the cardinal to conclude with the King. It did not take long for Lord Percy to 'fall in dalliance' with Queen Katherine's ladies. Although he got on well with them all, his favourite was Anne Boleyn.

Lancelott[5] has painted a bleak picture of life as a maid of honour in Queen Katherine's household. He describes a court without books, songs or dancing. He speaks of the ladies sitting in almost cloister-like silence with their sewing and tapestries, their days interrupted only by their carefully laid-down duties to the Queen and their strictly regulated mealtimes.

While this is not an entirely fair assessment of life in the service of Queen Katherine, it might be allowed that to someone of Anne's 'sprightly, volatile temperament', the Queen's court could have been a dull place indeed. We are reminded of the court of Queen Claude, the apparent lacklustre character and austerity of which has also been considered unsuited to Anne's cheery disposition. It naturally followed, then, that Anne would have welcomed the attentions of Lord Percy when he visited, entertaining the ladies as his master worked with the King in another part of the palace.

Not unexpectedly, perhaps, a secret love soon grew between the two young people and, according to Cavendish, it was not long before they 'were insured together'. Quite what Cavendish means by this term is not clear. It could mean that they had simply promised to marry some day or, at the other extreme, that they had entered into a formal pre-contract which, if consummated, would have been as legally binding as a marriage blessed by the church. Subsequent events would seem to suggest that it was closer to the latter, although whether or not it was consummated can never been known. As it was, any commitment made between Anne and Lord Percy would present a serious problem in view of Anne's projected marriage to James Butler. Whatever the case, whether by Percy's indiscretion, perhaps boasting that he had won the heart of the captivating Anne, or whether their secret had been betrayed by some tattler, King Henry soon found out about it and was less than pleased.

Cavendish puts the King's displeasure down to his own infatuation with Anne. In fact some historians accepted that Henry, seeing the woman who was to become his second wife and consort in the arms of Henry Percy, awoke to his true feelings about her. However, this was almost certainly not the case; the timing is far too early for that. Anne's romance with Henry Percy began in 1522, not long after her magnificent court debut. It would not reach its conclusion until the following year, although it would leave some serious and far-reaching consequences in its wake. By 1522, the King was very much involved with Anne's sister, Mary, who would continue to be the centre of his world for the next three years or so. Instead, Henry's disapproval can be explained by his interest in the continuing negotiations for the Percy-Talbot marriage as well as that between Anne and James Butler; he was keen to see each of these matches 'perfected'. The outcome, however, was the same. King Henry ordered Wolsey to speak to his wayward servant and put a stop to his nonsense.

Wolsey returned home to York Place, his residence at Westminster, which he held in virtue of his office as Archbishop of York. He called Percy to him and, in front of all the other servants, among them George Cavendish, he began to reproach the young page. He could not understand, he said, why Percy should become entangled with that foolish girl, Anne Boleyn. Percy should consider the great estate to which God had called him into the world, namely, his inheritance of the earldom of Northumberland, 'the most worthiest earldoms of this realm' upon the death of his father. As such, young Percy should have begged his father's consent before making such a rash commitment and, more importantly, informed the King of his intentions. King Henry, the cardinal assured Percy, would have shown his gratitude for such deference, but would also have proposed a much better match, one which not only would have better suited the young man's estate and honour, but also earned him the King's high estimation. As it was, Percy's imprudence had offended both his father and the King and had attached him to someone whom neither his king nor his father would have selected as a bride for him.

Wolsey then announced that he would send for Percy's father, the Earl of Northumberland, who would either break the contract between Percy and Anne or disinherit his son for ever. Northumberland would also hear the King's complaints about his son.

At this point, Cavendish refers once again to King Henry's interest in Anne, alleging that Henry had 'travelled already, and being almost at a point' with the Mistress Anne, although she was not yet aware of it. As noted, it is too premature at this period to look for early signs of Henry's infatuation with Anne Boleyn. However, some thirty-five years had passed between the unfolding of these events and Cavendish's committing them to paper, and allowance should be made for his fading memory regarding some of the smaller details. It appears that some of the finer points had converged in the mind of the former gentleman usher, which would account for the discrepancies.

Henry Percy heard his master out and then burst into tears. He told the cardinal that he had not known of his father's displeasure and was very sorry for having caused it. He pointed out, however, that he was of an age to take a wife of his own choosing, one of whom his father would have approved. He admitted that Anne was 'a simple maid, and having but a knight to her father', nevertheless, she was of good noble parentage. Percy then drew Wolsey's attention to Anne's descent from the Dukes of Norfolk on her mother's side and from the Earls of Ormond on her father's. Her status was, he noted, equal to his own once he inherited the earldom of Northumberland. Clearly, he and Anne had discussed family backgrounds, making Percy much better informed of Anne's heritage than his master was.

Certainly, there was no arguing with Lord Percy's reasoning. Perhaps he had been inexperienced enough to think he really could get away with taking a bride of his own choosing. Perhaps Anne, living up to her character of Perseverance, had persuaded her beloved that such a thing was possible if only the two of them held their nerve. Anne had, after all, witnessed similar behaviour while in France as a maid of honour to Mary Tudor, the French Queen. Mary had thrown all caution to the winds following the death of her husband, Louis XII, and had manipulated events to allow her to marry the man she had loved all along, Charles Brandon, Duke of Suffolk. Then, although it took a while, the couple had been forgiven and welcomed back at court, where Mary once more basked in the favour of her much-beloved brother. Interestingly, the man who had helped the couple back into King Henry's good graces had been Cardinal Wolsey himself. Perhaps Anne thought he would perform a similar service for her and Lord Percy once the fuss had died down. If so, she was mistaken.

It was possibly with the disagreeable memory of the Suffolk affair still clear in his mind that Wolsey turned to those gathered round and made some derisory comment about what conformity and wisdom there was in the young man's head. Certainly, the Duke and Duchess of Suffolk had managed to escape the wrath of the King, but they had the advantage of the duchess being Henry's adored sister and the duke being the royal favourite. With Henry Percy it was an entirely different matter. The boy was foolish to think that he would be allowed to have his own way in a matter as important as his marriage.

Turning back to Percy, the cardinal suggested to him that, since he had heard the King's intended pleasure regarding his projected marriage to Mistress Anne, he perhaps should relent. Percy retorted that the matter had gone so far, and before so many witnesses, that he did not know how he could break it off.

This assertion makes the probability that Anne and Henry Percy had done more than simply promised to marry high indeed. It really does seem that some formal commitment was made between them. Again, consummation would make such a commitment unbreakable, but such matters as go on behind closed doors depend solely upon the word of the two parties involved. In view of this the cardinal's exasperation is understandable. He could only assure Lord Percy that he would know what to do about it, as would the King. He added that when the Earl of Northumberland arrived the three of them would bring the whole business to a satisfactory conclusion. In the mean time, Percy was forbidden to see Anne again. With that, the cardinal rose and withdrew to his chamber.

It is possible that Cardinal Wolsey's vehemence in acting out the King's orders to part the wilful couple had a cause other than that of pleasing his master. It could equally be attributable to the resentment that existed between the cardinal and the Boleyns. This dated back at least to 1515 when Cardinal Wolsey had attempted to spoil relations between Thomas Boleyn and King Henry. Resentful of those who were close to the King, especially those whose opinions might be influential, Wolsey seemed deliberately to block Boleyn's advancement, depriving him of a post Henry had promised him. Furthermore, the cardinal's dislike of the Boleyns could also have been influenced by Thomas Boleyn's evangelical outlook, which could serve only to heighten Wolsey's defensiveness over attacks on the clergy that were currently taking place.[6]

As if this were not enough, Cardinal Wolsey also had difficulties with the Percys of Northumberland. The bad feeling had begun when Wolsey took up the archbishopric of York. Although he seldom, if ever, visited York, he did exercise great authority in the northern parts. This brought him into the sphere of the Percy family and relations were often less than genial. Wolsey, jealous of his power, saw Northumberland as a threat.[7] Moreover, his activities in this respect had the sanction of Henry. The King, worried about the ability of certain nobles to challenge royal authority, charged Wolsey to keep an eye on them. One such noble was Percy's father, the fifth Earl of Northumberland. This, and his resentment of the Boleyns, was all the excuse the cardinal needed to meddle with the blossoming love-affair between Anne Boleyn and Henry Percy.

Just as Wolsey had promised, the Earl of Northumberland was duly sent for. His first audience upon his arrival in London was with Cardinal Wolsey. It can be imagined with what delight the cardinal apprised him of his eldest son's behaviour. Now, it has been said that there was no love lost between the earl and his son, and Northumberland's subsequent behaviour towards the young man serves only to confirm this. After drinking a cup of wine with the cardinal, the earl was escorted towards the servant's quarters. Sitting down on a form provided for the use of the servers, he waited while his son was brought out to him.

Once again, the unlucky Lord Percy had to face the wrath of his superiors in the full view of his fellow servants. The earl opened with a devastating rebuke: 'Son, thou hast always been a proud, presumptuous, disdainful and a very unthrift waster, and even so hast thou declared thyself.' Northumberland berated the young man for treating him with so little regard and for not showing the King the deference and loyalty owing to him by all his subjects. Percy had acted in a manner inappropriate to the interests of his future estate. Once again, he was reminded that his promise to Anne Boleyn had incurred the King's displeasure, for which Northumberland and his posterity would be cast into 'utter subversion and dissolution' but for the good will of both King and Cardinal. If, therefore, Percy did not mend his ways the chance was great that he would be the last earl of their house. In this way, the future good conduct of the son was secured by the threat of his being disinherited by the father. Northumberland reminded his heir that he had two other sons between whom he could choose who would better succeed him.

Then, turning to the servants, who had been assembled to witness the scene, Northumberland declared that they might live to see the things of which he had spoken come true. In the mean time, he charged them to remain friends with his son and to point out his faults to him whenever he should go astray. Turning to Lord Percy once more, the earl ordered him to 'Go your ways, and attend upon my lord's grace your master, and see that you do your duty,' and so finishing, he rose and made his way to his barge.

Naturally, it was decided that the commitment Anne Boleyn and Henry Percy had made to each other should be dissolved. The proposed marriage between Percy and Mary Talbot was resurrected and negotiations recommenced. This was the last thing Percy wanted. He had no regard for Mary Talbot, nor she for him.

According to Cavendish, Anne's reaction to the news was, as might have been predicted, violent. Her fiery temper unleashed, she laid the blame firmly at Wolsey's door, vowing that, if it were ever in her power, she would get her revenge on the cardinal. Nevertheless, Cavendish asserts that Wolsey was not deserving of such wrath since he was merely carrying out the King's direct orders.

Henry Percy, then, was forbidden to see Anne. His marriage to Mary Talbot, although it would not take place for some time yet, was to all intents and purposes a *fait accompli*. The delay was caused by the legal niceties involved in disentangling Percy from the imprudent commitment he had made to Anne. For, even if it had not been consummated, a betrothal still had legal implications that had to be properly resolved before either party could marry elsewhere. This was eventually accomplished, but only after 'long debating and consultation'.[8] It then required only to add the finishing touches to the negotiations and to draw up a contract of marriage that would satisfy the Earls of Northumberland and Shrewsbury, if not their children.

Anne, her suitor forbidden to her, is commonly believed to have left court soon afterwards. Bishop Burnet[9] states that she went to France, where she returned to the service of Queen Claude, and did not come back to England until 1527. In this, he is clearly mistaken, since Queen Claude died in 1524. Also the political situation that had coincided with Anne's return to England during the winter of 1521–22, had not improved sufficiently to allow her to return to the French court.

Agnes Strickland[10] insists that Anne had been dismissed from court, punished by the King for having preferred young Percy to him. Following Cavendish, she states that Anne went to her father's house at Hever where, according to the former gentleman usher, she 'smoked'. By this he means that Anne fumed, was consumed by her anger.

This is also the opinion of Lancelott[11] who maintains that Henry acquainted Thomas Boleyn with what had been going on while he was away in Spain on the King's business. Sir Thomas had then rebuked Anne for her disobedience before withdrawing her from the court. Left to seethe in the quiet solitude of Hever, Anne had no idea that her rustication was to hide the fact that Henry was in love with her; a secret that had been kept even from her father. As such, Anne really had been sent to the country as punishment for accepting Lord Percy's suit.

However, Lancelott continues, it was not long before the King showed his true feelings. Henry, using any excuse he could think of, made secret and unexpected visits to Hever. If he had come to see Anne, his efforts went unrewarded. She had been shut up in her chamber, her father telling the King that she was indisposed. Disappointed, the King quickly left.

This story, with its heroine shut away in a tower to keep her away from an unsuitable admirer is very romantic, but untrue.

Nevertheless, it is almost certain that Henry was a regular visitor to Hever at this time, and his visits would have been clandestine. This was due to his romantic involvment with Anne's elder sister, Mary. They often used Penshurst Place, close to Hever, for their trysts but there is nothing to say that Henry did not visit his beloved at her family home on occasion. However, since contemporary sources are silent on the matter, it cannot be said for certain that Anne actually did return to Hever, although it is probable that she did.

Meanwhile, the negotiations for Anne's projected marriage to James Butler had not yet reached their conclusion. As it was, Thomas Boleyn and Piers Butler continued to drag their feet. Whatever problems they encountered or caused, no agreement could be reached that was satisfactory to both parties. The delay in reaching an agreement has been attributed to Sir Piers' excessive demands, which would not have found sympathy with Anne's notoriously grasping father.

However, it is equally possible that Sir Thomas Boleyn was not as enthusiastic about the Butler alliance as he might have been. He might have preferred to marry his daughter to Henry Percy, seeing him as a more desirable son-in-law. It is easy to see why. The Percys, despite their flagging fortunes, were still an important family. As the premier family in the North Country, their return to their former glory was almost inevitable, especially with Thomas Boleyn guiding the King on their behalf. Traditionally holders of the wardenship of the eastern and middle marches towards

Scotland, they would have carried out important duties on behalf of the crown.

For Anne, life as the Countess of Northumberland would have been spent at the magnificent Percy castles of Alnwick, Walkworth and Bamburgh. There were castles in Yorkshire too, among them Spofforth, near Wetherby and Wressell, about seven miles east of Selby. The Percys also owned two mansions in London's Newington Green, one on the north side, the other on the south. This was a favourite hunting area during Tudor times and, no doubt, well known to King Henry. A Percy alliance would allow Thomas Boleyn to remain in touch with his favourite daughter, something the match with the Irish James Butler would have made difficult.

If this were indeed Sir Thomas's thinking, he had time on his side. He had spent the period from October 1522 to May of the following year on a diplomatic mission to Spain. His absence did little to help further his negotiations with Piers Butler. It can easily be seen, then, why Sir Piers gave up on the idea and walked away. In an instant Anne's semi-betrothal to James Butler was ended.

Shortly after this, in January or February 1524, Anne's hopes of marriage to Henry Percy, shattered as they had been by Cardinal Wolsey acting on behalf of King Henry, ended for good when his earlier betrothal to Mary Talbot was revived. Now, despite her strong connections to the court of Henry VIII, where courtly love, with its love sighs, poetry and chivalry played such an important role, Anne Boleyn now found herself strangely alone.

'Where Force and Beauty Met': Anne & Thomas Wyatt 1524–1526

Anne's whereabouts and activities following the end of the Percy affair must remain a mystery. If she had been rusticated, retreating to her father's home at Hever, it is not known when she returned to court. If she had continued at court, but remained beyond history's notice, there is no indication of what might have brought her back into royal favour. Received wisdom insists that Anne was indeed taken to Hever by her father following the breaking of her relationship with Henry Percy. Similarly, it is believed that she returned to court at some point during 1525. What is certain is that, at some point after her failed liaison with Henry Percy, Anne became involved in some way with Thomas Wyatt.

Thomas Wyatt, the gentle and romantic poet, diplomat and man of action, was said to have lost his heart to Anne the moment she first appeared at court early in 1522. This would mean that he was pursuing Anne at the same time that she was being courted by Henry Percy. However, the timing of her association with Thomas Wyatt, as with much else to do with their relationship, is open to conjecture. Who, then, was this new man is Anne's life?

Although popularly associated with the county of Kent, the Wyatts were in fact of old Yorkshire stock. The family originated in Southange, today South Haigh near Kexbrough in the Parish of Darton.

Unusually for a Yorkshireman, Sir Henry Wyatt, Thomas's father, was a supporter of the Lancastrian cause during the Wars of the Roses. It is possible that he participated in the Duke of Buckingham's unsuccessful rebellion against King Richard III during the autumn of 1483. Family legend has it that Sir Henry was imprisoned and tortured by King Richard himself and that, during his imprisonment, he was fed by a cat who brought pigeons to him. Whatever the truth of it, Bosworth liberated Sir Henry, who was shown great favour by the new King, Henry VII. He was appointed clerk of the King's jewels in September 1486 and became master of the King's jewels two years later. At the same time, he held the post of clerk of the royal mint. In 1494, he became assayer of money and coinage and was elevated to the post of comptroller of the royal mint.

In 1502, Sir Henry married Anne Skinner, a daughter of John Skinner, esquire, of Reigate in Surrey. Since her husband's work frequently took him away from the family home, Lady Wyatt kept an open house, taking in waifs and strays and offering hospitality to weary travellers. One visitor was the abbot of the nearby abbey of Boxley who, despite the kindness of his hostess, saw fit to take advantage of one of her maids. Caught in a compromising position, the abbot was escorted outside the gates of the castle by the outraged Lady Wyatt. Then, without the benefit of an ecclesiastical court, he was unceremoniously dumped in the stocks before the local gentry and peasantry.

Sir Henry was approached by the council about his wife's behaviour, but all he had to say was that, if he or any of them had acted as the abbot had done, he would fully expect her to punish them in the same way. He added that, if the lords wished him to be responsible for his wife's actions, they should allow him to live in the country with her. Moreover, as he pointed out to them: 'If you... should seem to allow the abbot to play with my wife's maids, will not your wives think that you love the sport yourselves, and allow yourselves as great a liberty?' His point was well taken and Lady Wyatt's chastisement of the abbot was passed over.[1]

The scene of the abbot of Boxley's indecorous handling was the beautiful Allington Castle on the Medway, just north of Maidstone in Kent, which Sir Henry Wyatt had acquired in 1492. While the family were to maintain its links with Yorkshire, Allington was now their principal home. It was almost certainly here, in 1503, that Thomas, the eldest of the three surviving children of Sir Henry and Anne, was born. Thomas Wyatt, then, was the first of the Wyatts of Kent.

A legend of Thomas's early life features a lion whelp and a greyhound, which his father had bought and kept as pets at Allington. Like many faithful animals, they would prowl the gates or the hall while their master was away, awaiting his return, when they would leap on him in enthusiastic welcome. One day, the lion whelp, having grown in size and strength, roared at Sir Henry as he entered his castle, flying at him and knocking him to the ground. The greyhound, in a bid to save its master, pounced at the lion, sinking its teeth into the woolly mane. Thomas, hearing the commotion, rushed out, drew his sword and plunged it into the lion's heart. In time to come, when Thomas Wyatt found his place at King Henry's court, the King would say of the poet, 'Oh, he can tame lions!'[2] Henry VIII, who liked to consider himself the lion of England, no doubt applied a double meaning to his words.

Thomas was a precocious child. In 1515, at the age of only twelve, he went up to St John's College Cambridge, the great centre of humanist learning in England. He did not take a degree, as is often believed, but it was probably here that his love for Horace, Seneca and Epictetus was awakened.

The following year, he and his friend and neighbour, Thomas Poynings, served as ewerers at the christening of Princess Mary. Then, at the age of seventeen, Thomas was married to Elizabeth Brooke, daughter of Thomas Brooke, eighth Baron Cobham. A son was born to the couple in 1521 and named Thomas after his father. However, this happy event concealed a poignant reality. The Wyatt marriage was a disaster. Elizabeth was an adulteress; Thomas, by his own admission, was not altogether blameless himself. If the imperial ambassador, Chapuys, is to be believed, the couple had separated by the mid-1520s.[3]

Thomas Wyatt's marriage might have been a source of great unhappiness, but he was beginning to carve out a successful career at court. In 1524, he followed in his father's footsteps by becoming clerk of the King's jewels. Like the other young men who surrounded King Henry, Thomas liked nothing better than pageantry and display. On one occasion, he took part in the pageant of the Castle of Loyalty, which was held as part of the Christmas revels in 1524–25. Several of the court gallants had petitioned the King for permission to hold a pageant. Henry had gladly given his consent, perhaps seeing it as an opportunity to show off his own skills before the Scottish ambassadors, who were visiting the court.

A castle was built in the tiltyard at Greenwich. It was a huge construction, with each wall measuring some twenty feet in length and fifty feet high. It was well defended on the north and south sides by dykes crossed by two drawbridges, while a huge bank protected the west side. It was said to have been impenetrable, but King Henry thought differently and ordered an assault on the castle.

As the six men-at-arms emerged from the castle, they saw two elderly knights being led into the tiltyard by two ladies dressed in purple damask and riding palfreys. The ladies escorted the ancient knights to where Queen Katherine and her ladies were sitting and asked if the knights might present a bill to her. The Queen kindly agreed. The knights explained that youth had left them and age had come, and this would prevent their taking part in feats of arms. However, courage, desire and good will remained and urged them to break spears, which they would gladly do if the Queen would give them licence. Katherine and her ladies praised the courage of the two old knights and gladly granted them their licence.

At this the two knights cast off their robes. To the astonishment of the entire court they revealed themselves as the King and the Duke of Suffolk. Their costumes were of cloth of gold 'very curiously' embroidered with purple, silver and black. Several men followed, one of whom was Thomas Wyatt. Each man ran eight courses during which King Henry broke seven spears, while the Scottish ambassadors, as expected, praised his skill and courage.

Thomas Wyatt was strikingly handsome, with short, wavy hair, a long, flowing beard and soft eyes behind which burned intelligent and intellectual fires. Tall, well-built and athletic, chivalrous and romantic, his friend and fellow bard Henry, Earl of Surrey, described him as one 'where force and beauty met', and that when nature made him she lost the mould.[4] The anonymous writer of the *Chronicle of King Henry VIII of England* stated that 'there was no prettier man at Court than he was'.[5] Women were naturally attracted to Wyatt and it is possible that Anne Boleyn was one of them.

It is often thought that Anne and Thomas had known each other in childhood. Certainly, this might be expected. Their fathers had shared the governorship of Norwich Castle since 1511, and the two families lived within twenty miles of each other. However, such an early acquaintance is by no means certain. Thomas was only ten years old when Anne left England for Margaret of Austria's court in the Low Countries. Then there is George Wyatt's assertion that Thomas first became aware of Anne when she came to court. Thomas, instantly attracted to her, was said to be 'surprised by the sight thereof'.[6] Of course, this could refer to the adult Anne, whom he now looked upon for the first time.

Whether or not Anne was one of the ladies who had accompanied Queen Katherine to the pageant of the Castle of Loyalty is impossible to say because they are not named. She was certainly a member of the Queen's household at the time. Following the excitement of the day's entertainments at the tiltyard, the Queen's ladies danced at the mask that formed part of the evening festivities. Again, the ladies are not named, but it would be strange to think that Anne, whose dancing had already earned her much admiration and praise, was not one of them. Perhaps Thomas found himself partnering the captivating brunette and, like his King in the not too distant future, found himself struck with the dart of love.

At the time of the Castle of Loyalty, King Henry was still very much involved with Anne Boleyn's sister, Mary. However, as the heat of the summer mellowed into a cool, crisp autumn, their once passionate relationship came to an end. Mary was pregnant with her second child by this time. Although Henry had taken her back following the birth of a daughter the previous year, it soon became clear that he would not do so again. Mary returned to her husband, giving birth to a son on 4 March 1526. In the mean season, Henry began his search for a new mistress.

In fact, Henry seems to have been quite certain that he had already found the lady who would replace Mary Boleyn in his heart and, he hoped, his bed. For those with eyes to see, he proclaimed the fact that he had found a new love at the joust, which was held as part of the Shrovetide festivities of 1526.

The joust was held at the tiltyard at Greenwich. The King led on one side and the Marquis of Exeter on the other. Henry was resplendent in cloth of gold and silver, richly embroidered with a man's heart gripped in a press and engulfed in flames. The motto read *declare ie nose* – 'declare I dare not'. As was usual upon such occasions, the joust was followed by a feast for the pleasure of the Queen and her ladies. Henry's enigmatic message, which he dared not declare, was that his new love was none other than the sister of his former mistress, Anne Boleyn.

It is not known whether Thomas Wyatt attended this event. He was probably still in England at this point, although it is possible that he was already making preparations for a journey to France. For, in April 1526, he embarked on his first diplomatic mission abroad.

Thomas Wyatt and Sir Thomas Chaney had been sent to congratulate François I on his release from captivity by the Emperor Charles and to negotiate England's position relative to the League of Cognac. Wyatt arrived back in England towards the end of May, having been sent by Cheney to carry news of the mission to Wolsey. Within a few weeks, the court left for its summer progress, from which the King and his entourage returned in October 1526.

Anne Boleyn did not spend the summer with the court. It could be that she had not been asked to accompany her mistress on the summer progress. On the other hand, it is more probable that Anne voluntarily withdrew from the court, wearied by Henry's increasingly heavy-handed attempts to court her. It was at this point, in the late summer or early autumn of 1526, that the story of Anne Boleyn and Thomas Wyatt appears to have begun.

When Thomas Wyatt asserted that he 'could gladly yield to be tied for ever with the knot of her love',[7] did he have Anne in mind? It seems not, at least in this case. The object of his love is described in this verse as having hair of 'crisped gold', quite the opposite of Anne, whose hair was dark and sleek.

Nevertheless, those who would seek evidence of a love affair between Thomas and Anne usually appeal to Wyatt's beautiful poetry. The entire canon is pored over for signs that this poem or that sonnet was inspired by Anne or dedicated to her. Of all the poems written by Thomas Wyatt, only a handful can be linked to Anne Boleyn. Even here, though, the link is not always entirely convincing. One such poem is:

> What wourde is that that chaungeth not,
> Though it be tourned and made in twain?
> It is myn aunswer, god it wot,
> And eke the only causer of my payn;
> A love that rewardeth with disdain
> Yet it is loved. What will ye more?
> It is my helth eke and my sore.[8]

The poem offers the reader a riddle, the answer to which is, of course, 'Anna'. Indeed, in some versions of this poem the line, 'It is myn aunswer, god it wot,' is changed to 'It is mine Anna, God it wot'.[9] In either case, it is generally supposed that Wyatt wrote the poem about Anne Boleyn, a somewhat bold conclusion, since he could have had another Anne in mind.

Another poem, later given the title 'The Lover Confesseth Him in Love with Phyllis', begins with the line 'If waker care, if sudden pale colour'. It contains the following lines:

> If thou ask whom: sure since I did refrain
> Brunet, that set my wealth in such a roar,
> The unfeigned cheer of Phyllis hath the place
> That Brunet had: she hath, and ever shall:
> She from my self now hath me in her grace:
> She hath in hand my wit, my will, and all:
> My heart alone well worthy she doth stay,
> Without whose help scant do I live a day.[10]

The Brunet, whose place has now been taken by Phyllis is, again, believed to be Anne Boleyn. Anne, of course, could accurately be referred to as a brunette. Also, the line: 'Brunet, that set my wealth in such a roar' originally read: 'Brunet, that set my country in such a roar'. In the sixteenth century, the term 'country' was frequently used to mean 'county'. This change, which is in Wyatt's own hand, was possibly made to refer to Anne's home county of Kent, which was also Thomas Wyatt's home county. Consequently, Anne set the county of Kent in a roar, but also the country as a whole.

However, the 'Brunet' of this poem could just as easily be Wyatt's wife, Elizabeth Brooke. It is not known what colour her hair was, but Elizabeth was also a woman of Kent and she did set Wyatt's wealth – his wellbeing – as well as his county in a roar, if we accept 'roar' to refer to their tumultuous marriage.

Still, it is not necessary to appeal to Thomas Wyatt's verses for evidence that he and Anne Boleyn were involved in some way. The chroniclers thought they knew the answer. According to the *Chronicle of King Henry VIII of England*, Thomas Wyatt visited Anne's home, presumably Hever, one night while her parents were away at court. Having let himself in, he made his way upstairs to her chamber to find her in bed. Startled by her unexpected visitor, Anne asked him what he was doing there, it being such a late hour. Wyatt explained that his love for her was so great that he could not keep away, but had been forced out of passion to seek consolation.

With that, Wyatt approached Anne and, somewhat boldly, kissed her. Anne said nothing, nor did she push him away. Encouraged, Thomas touched her breasts, those 'pretty duckys' that would so entrance King Henry in the not too distant future. Again, Anne made no attempt to stop him, which encouraged the poet to take even greater liberties.

As Wyatt began to undress he was startled by a great stamping that came from the chamber above. Anne hurried out of bed, grabbing a skirt as she went, and left her room by a staircase which led up behind the bed. Thomas remained, waiting for her for over an hour. Upon her return, however, Anne refused to let him touch her. He left then but within a week her reluctance had evaporated and Thomas Wyatt received the 'consolation' he had so eagerly sought. As to Anne's sudden disappearance, the poet assumed that she had a lover hidden upstairs and that the stamping had been a signal for her to go to him.

The story of Thomas Wyatt's visit to Hever is not entirely charming or romantic. The poet, fevered with passion, visits his beloved one dark night seeking solace from his pains. That he was able to let himself into Anne's home, and that he knew where her bedroom was, hints that there was already a degree of intimacy between the two. However, their relationship was not exclusive. Anne, somewhat unsympathetic to Thomas on this occasion, had another lover, who was even then preparing himself to receive her upon his signal. Another time she is responsive to Thomas, allowing him his yearned-for consolation.

How much of this story is true? Even at first reading it is clear that it owes more than a little to Boccaccio's *The Decameron*. However, whatever its source of inspiration, the tale does point to contemporary belief in a connection of some sort between Anne Boleyn and Thomas Wyatt. The story does not suggest a date or time period for this relationship, but it does place it prior to Henry's involvement with Anne. The narrative also requires Anne's absence from court. As a result, it fits in with what can be deduced concerning Anne's whereabouts during the latter months of 1526. It was during this period that Anne had returned to Hever in order to escape Henry's persistent and, at that point, unwelcome courtship.

Another narrative, in which a relationship between Anne and Thomas is described, comes from the pen of Thomas's grandson, George Wyatt. Here we find the poet entertaining Anne as she sat at her needlework one day. Thomas was in a playful mood so that when he noticed a jewel hanging by a lace from her pocket, he snatched it and thrust it into his bosom, refusing to give it back. Delighted with his trophy, he wore it round his neck, thinking that he would have it with her blessing or that it would provide an occasion for her to speak to him again.

Unbeknown to Wyatt, his activities were being closely watched by King Henry. The King had developed a fancy for Anne, although it was still very much a secret at that point. Nevertheless, Henry had already made it his business to find out whether Anne was chaste or whether her character was stained. To his delight, he found that her reputation was above reproach and he sought to press his suit with a view to marrying her. With hope in his heart, the mighty King approached the Lady Anne with this proposition which, he was delighted to find, was graciously received. Henry accepted a ring from her, which he proudly wore on his little finger.

A few days later, the King was playing bowls with some of his favourites, one of whom was Thomas Wyatt. Suddenly a dispute arose over a shot. Wyatt claimed that it was his, while the King insisted that it was not. Merrily, Henry then pointed to the wood with the finger upon which he wore Anne's ring and said, 'Wyatt, I tell thee it is mine.' Wyatt, his eyes falling upon the ring, answered, 'If it may like your majesty to give me leave to measure it, I hope it will be mine', upon which he took the jewel from round his neck and proceeded to use the ribbon to measure the cast. The King recognized the jewel as having once belonged to Anne. His mood darkened as he said, 'It may be so, but then I am deceived', and with that he broke up the game. Henry later confronted Anne with the fact that he had seen Thomas Wyatt with her jewel. Anne gently explained how the poet had come by it and the King at last understood that Thomas posed no threat to him.

This little anecdote clearly owes much to the traditions of courtly love. Also, it is resonant with a similar game played by Charles Brandon with the Archduchess Margaret, in which Brandon took a ring and refused to return it until she gave him another.

George Wyatt's anecdote expects the reader to believe that Henry had already taken it into his head to marry Anne at such an early phase in their relationship. It also overlooks the fact that, while Henry's desire for Anne is still a secret at this point, Wyatt knew enough about it to challenge the King.

Notwithstanding all this, there might be more than a grain of truth to the account. It is entirely possible that the story reflects what the court remembered about Henry's interest in Anne at this point, how it interpreted the opening stages of their relationship. George Wyatt's story does hint at some degree of association between Anne Boleyn and Thomas Wyatt. In addition, as with the *Chronicle of King Henry VIII of England*, Wyatt was not Anne's only suitor. Whereas in the *Chronicle* Wyatt's rival is not identified, here we see that he is none other than King Henry.

The idea of a romance between Anne Boleyn and Thomas Wyatt was a perennial favourite among the Catholic community, both in England and abroad. The story, as it appears in the *Chronicle*, is one manifestation of the Catholic community's fascination for, and hatred of, Anne. The source for the story was probably the Spanish community in London. As a consequence, its primary concern was for Queen Katherine's cause which, it was probably felt, could be further served by the blackening of Anne's name. Thomas Wyatt's reputation as *homme à femme* lent the story a certain credibility, adding further weight and giving it the firm foundation of historical fact. Other Catholic writers took up the tale and developed it further. One of these was Nicholas Harpsfield.

Perhaps best known for *The Life and Death of Sir Thomas Moore, Knight*, Nicholas Harpsfield also wrote a scathing attack on Archbishop Thomas Cranmer. *Cranmer's Recantacyons* is, effectively, a character assassination of the archbishop set within the context of his imprisonment, trial and execution. Apparently not satisfied with his first effort, Harpsfield revisited the subject in another book, *A Treatise on the Pretended Divorce*. Cranmer was a prime target for such scorn because he was held responsible for the calamity that had fallen upon Katherine of Aragon and her daughter, Mary. It was during Mary's reign that Harpsfield was writing. Almost by default, then, Anne Boleyn became the villainess of the piece and Harpsfield lost no opportunity to portray her as such. His weapon of choice was Thomas Wyatt.

According to Harpsfield,[11] Thomas Wyatt, hearing that King Henry wished to marry Anne Boleyn, sought to dissuade him. Anne, he said, is 'not meet to be coupled with your grace', explaining that Anne was given to loose and base conversation (association). This was something Wyatt knew from experience because he had known Anne carnally. Astonished, Henry mused awhile on what the poet had told him before he replied, 'Wyatt, thou hast done like an honest men [sic], yet I charge thee make no more words of this matter to any man living.'

Harpsfield, then, shows Henry refusing to believe Wyatt's story of Anne's lack of morals. The author's method is to take a detail from the case of Katherine Howard, Henry's fifth wife, who was executed for treasonous adultery. Henry had similarly refused to believe in Katherine's guilt until he was presented with incontrovertible proof. The significance of Katherine Howard to Harpsfield, however, was that she was found guilty of her crime despite Henry's original estimate of the affair. Harpsfield seeks to show that, since Henry was wrong about Katherine, he was equally wrong about Anne.

Such a literary device, in which a historically accurate detail is incorporated into a dubious account, is a well-used technique. It lends authenticity to the narrative, conferring upon it a degree of authority and acting as a hook to draw in and sway readers. However, should any misgivings remain, Harpsfield points out that, since he had his story from Anthony Bonvisi, it is trustworthy. Perhaps. Bonvisi might have been a trustworthy man, but was he objective?

One of Anthony Bonvisi's friends was Thomas Runcorn, Archdeacon of Bangor and a former chaplain to Cardinal Wolsey.

Runcorn was at least acquainted with Thomas Wyatt,[12] and might have had access to information about certain events within the poet's life that others could only speculate upon.

Similarly, Bonvisi knew Henry Percy. On 7 July 1531, Percy granted the honour of Cockermouth, as well as all his other Cumberland estates to Henry VIII in return for the quashing of bonds worth £8,062 contracted by the earl on behalf of Anthony Bonvisi, described as a 'failed Italian merchant'.[13] Yet another common acquaintance between Thomas Wyatt and Bonvisi was Thomas Cromwell. It is clear, then, that Bonvisi was in a position to be well informed about the men in the life of Anne Boleyn.

On the other hand, Anthony Bonvisi was a firm friend to Thomas More and Bishop John Fisher. More, who had known Bonvisi for some forty years, called him 'the apple of myne eye' and spoke of his being not a guest, but 'a continual nurseling' in Bonvisi's home. It is believed that their conversations helped inspire More's *Utopia*.[14]

Bonvisi shared More's and Fisher's opposition to King Henry's attempts to annul his marriage to Queen Katherine. He supported them during their imprisonment in the Tower, bringing them food, wine and, for More, a silk camlet gown to wear to his execution. Settling at Louvain shortly after the accession of Edward VI, Bonvisi's home became a refuge for Catholic exiles. Many of these included members of More's family, as well as Nicholas Harpsfield. Their thinking, which fed upon the anecdotes and traditions that informed such works as the *Chronicle of King Henry VIII of England* and led to the writing of *A Treatise on the Pretended Divorce* and other such books, is all too obvious. While Harpsfield provides a useful source, he should be approached with caution by those who would appeal to his work for research material on Anne Boleyn.

Another work that came from the recusant Catholic stable is *The Rise and Growth of the Anglican Schism* by Nicholas Sander. Younger than Bonvisi and Harpsfield, Sander also lived at Louvain for a while, matriculating from the university in November 1564. By the time he came to write the *Schism*, he was living in exile at Rome, having been unable to return to his native England due to Queen Elizabeth's presence on the throne. He had already made it his business to take every opportunity to slander Elizabeth. In the *Schism* Sander took the attack from a different angle, focusing upon the Queen's mother, Anne Boleyn, against whom his religious affiliations made him naturally prejudiced.

Sander[15] begins his account of Anne's iniquity by rehearsing the story in which Thomas Wyatt discovered that the King had fallen in love with Anne Boleyn and wished to marry her. Wyatt was afraid of the consequences to him if the details of Anne's shameless life came out and it was discovered that he had not disclosed what he knew. Wyatt thought that the best course of action was to confess all; not to the King this time, but to the council. He admitted to having sinned with Anne Boleyn, never imagining that King Henry would one day want to make her his wife.

The council, having listened to what Wyatt had to say, pointed out that they were duty bound to watch over the honour and good name of the King as well as his life. In addition, it was the opinion of them all that Anne Boleyn was stained in her reputation, and so publicly, that it was unseemly for Henry to marry her. With that, certain members of the council were sent to the King to acquaint him with the unpleasant truth about his beloved.

As with Harpsfield, Sander tells his readers that Henry fell silent upon hearing the news of Anne's indiscretions. He then spoke. He began by assuring the council members that he was aware that they had acted out of respect and affection for him. Nevertheless, he continued, he regarded such stories as the invention of wicked men. He added, for good measure, that he could affirm upon oath that Anne was 'a woman of the purest life'.

The King's response reached Thomas Wyatt, who was greatly angered by this slur upon his integrity. He returned to the council, telling them that he would show the King proof Anne's guilt; for Anne Boleyn was passionately in love with Wyatt.

The poet's words were once again conveyed to Henry, this time by the King's closest friend, Charles Brandon. As before, Henry dismissed the accusation. He informed Brandon that he had no desire to see anything of the kind, for Wyatt was a bold villain and not to be trusted. Once again, then, a particular feature from the story of the fall of Katherine Howard is used to demonstrate Henry's implacable but misplaced faith in Anne, as Sander saw it.

It was Sander's mistreatment of Anne's memory that prompted George Wyatt to write 'The Life of Queen Anne Boleigne'. Encouraged in his endeavours by Matthew Parker, Wyatt's study is, in part, a polemic against Sander's work. 'The Life of Queen

Anne Boleigne' is a eulogistic discourse in defence of the late Queen. Perhaps for that reason it, as with the Catholic accounts, should be approached with caution by scholars of Anne Boleyn. However, George Wyatt was the grandson of Thomas Wyatt, and much of what is contained in this work probably came to him through family tradition and, in at least one instance, eye-witness testimony.

When looked at as a whole, and when allowances are made for bias towards one side or the other, these various accounts do point to some relationship between Anne Boleyn and Thomas Wyatt. Certainly, their contemporaries thought a connection had existed otherwise the story contained in the *Chronicle of King Henry VIII of England* would not have found a foothold, let alone inspired further, still more slanderous tales. In the case of Harpsfield, there could be more behind his narrative than simple conjecture fuelled by the desire to darken Anne's memory. A romance between Anne and Thomas Wyatt provides the main focus of each narrative, with the looming presence of King Henry casting a shadow over whatever love might have grown between the two.

Nevertheless, it is possible that Thomas Wyatt had no romantic feelings at all for Anne, but simply used her as one of his muses. His poems are filled with expressions of the agony of unrequited love and of cruel mistresses. On the other hand, he could have loved Anne passionately, indulging in poetic licence to 'link' himself with a woman whom he could woo from the relative safety of the traditions of courtly love so beloved at the Tudor court.

The reality is probably somewhere in between these two extremes. Nevertheless, any emotional involvement on Wyatt's part appears not to have been reciprocated. As George Wyatt explains, Anne, seeing that the poet was married, 'rejected all his speech of love'.[16] This is understandable. Anne had already been through a difficult time as a result of her relationship with Henry Percy. Her former love had recently married and was now beyond her reach forever. Thomas Wyatt had been a pleasing diversion, but Anne probably was not anxious to embark upon another relationship that could lead nowhere.

Instead, as George Wyatt suggests, Anne not only enjoyed the flattering attention of Thomas, she also made use of it. The poet, she knew, was held in high esteem by other men and his interest in her would stimulate a similar response in them. In this way she could attract the attention of a man with whom she could enjoy the full pleasures of a romance and who would, perhaps, make her a suitable husband. If so, once Henry cast his eye upon the intriguing and exotic maid of honour, Anne got more than she bargained for.

As it was, Thomas Wyatt knew that he had no chance with Anne. Although his interest in her coincided with the breakdown of his marriage, he had nothing to offer her other than to make her his mistress. For someone who might have been a countess to an attractive and reliable Irish chieftain or even the future Countess of Northumberland, the idea of becoming the mistress of a mere gentleman, however charming he might be, was simply unacceptable.

The conclusion of Thomas Wyatt's flirtation with Anne is best illustrated in the poet's own words in what is arguably his most famous poem:

Whoso list to hunt? I know where is an hind!
But as for me, alas! I may no more,
The vain travail hath wearied me so sore;
I am of them that furthest come behind,
Yet may I by no means my wearied mind,
Draw from the deer; but as she fleeth afore
Fainting I follow; I leave off therefore,
Since in a net I seek to hold the wind.
Who list her hunt, I put him out of doubt
As well as I, may spend his time in vain!
And graven with diamonds in letters plain,
There is written her fair neck round about;
'*Noli me tangere*; for Caesar's I am,
And wild for to hold, though I seem tame.'[17]

Wyatt had cultivated a love for the Italian poets, among them Petrarch. The inspiration for 'Whoso list to hunt' was Petrarch's sonnet 'Una candida cerva', of which it is, in part, a translation.

The words *noli me tangere* occur in the Gospel of John 20.17. The newly resurrected Jesus urges his first witness, Mary, not to touch him because he has not yet ascended to his Father. The meaning of Jesus' words is that his disciples should not try to hold on to him, but rather to let him go. This is suggestive of a religious dimension to the poem, but there is more to it than that. Thomas Wyatt explains that he was merely one of many who were hunting the hind. Since he was one of those that had 'furthest come behind', he not only knew he had little chance of success in catching her, he also appears to have been somewhat unenthusiastic about attempting to do so. He then goes on to say that he withdrew from the hunt when he saw that the quarry was being pursued by another.

One of the underlying themes here, for Wyatt, is release. Faced with an object of desire that he finds to be unavailable to him, he feels he has no option but to let it go and allow it to be taken by its rightful owner. Translated to Anne Boleyn, Thomas Wyatt stepped aside when it became obvious that he had a rival for her affection. Henry VIII had 'noticed' Anne, obliging Wyatt to withdraw his suit. Now the 'property' of Caesar, King Henry, Anne was untouchable: *noli me tangere*.

Thomas Wyatt left England again on 7 January 1527. This time he travelled with Sir John Russell to the papal court. Wyatt's decision to accompany Russell was, according to one account, a hasty one. Sir John had already embarked upon his journey and was sailing past Greenwich when he encountered Thomas Wyatt on the riverbank. The poet asked Russell where he was going, to which the reply was: 'To Italy, sent by the King'. Wyatt then said, 'And I… will, if you please, ask leave, get money, and go with you.' Russell, delighted to have Wyatt's company, answered, 'No man more welcome'. They then set off together on what was to be something of an adventure.[18]

It is possible that seeing Thomas Wyatt court this captivating woman had alerted feelings of envy in Henry who, selfishly, wanted to possess her for himself. On the other hand, it is more than probable that Henry had already noticed Anne. In this scenario, it would be acceptable to speculate that his feelings for her crystallized, taking on new intensity when he saw one of his courtiers encroaching on what he had now come to consider his own territory.

Thomas Wyatt, once he saw that the King had staked his claim, stood down and allowed Henry a clear field. Perhaps to forget Anne, perhaps simply to get out of the way, the young poet left England, embarking on a mission to Italy. The way was now clear for Henry to make his move.

It would, perhaps, be interesting, as a postscript to this chapter, to note the similarities that existed between Thomas Wyatt and Henry VIII. Both men showed an interest in Anne, although how far Thomas Wyatt was allowed to go in expressing his affection can, as with Henry Percy, only be guessed. Both King Henry and Thomas Wyatt were married at the time they had become involved with Anne, and both were fathers: Henry to a daughter, Wyatt to a son. Nevertheless, Thomas Wyatt, even if his love had been reciprocated, would never have been able to offer Anne anything other than to make her his mistress. Henry VIII was in a similar position. However, the King, unlike the poet, had the power to overturn religious and political convention. He would change the entire complexion of England and expose his kingdom and his people to enormous peril in order to have the woman he loved.

7

Anne's Revenge 1527–1530

The Spanish ambassador, Inigo de Mendoza, wrote on 26 October 1527 that,

> the said lady [Anne], to whom the King is much attached, bears
> the Legate [Wolsey] a grudge on account of his having some years
> since deprived her father of a high official post which he held here,
> as well as because she has discovered that during his last visit to
> France the Legate proposed to have an alliance for the King of
> England found in that country.[1]

George Cavendish, on the other hand, as he relates the story of Anne's relationship with Henry Percy, asserts that she had been greatly offended by Cardinal Wolsey, whom she had blamed for the break-up of their affair. Cavendish notes that Anne had threatened Wolsey, saying that, 'if it lay ever in her power, she would work the cardinal as much displeasure'. This, according to Cavendish, is the origin of the long-held belief that Anne Boleyn had become the great enemy of the cardinal and that, from that point on, she had plotted his downfall.

Cavendish ought to have known better. As has been shown, Wolsey had his own motives for sabotaging the Percy-Boleyn match quite apart from obeying the King's orders. However, Cavendish's position on this point can be explained by the fact that, at the time of writing, the throne was occupied by Queen Mary. Anne Boleyn was very much held responsible for the calamity that had shattered the Queen's early life: the annulment of her mother's marriage to King Henry and her own subsequent illegitimacy. As such, Anne was also held responsible for Wolsey's fall, with the cardinal being depicted as yet another victim of Anne's selfishness and ambition.

Perhaps, also, it should be allowed that, after so many years, and with the distorted view that hindsight can so often afford, Cavendish simply saw in the course of earlier events the seeds of later ones. This occurs also in the instance of Percy's being called a wastrel, as well as the threat of his being the last Earl of Northumberland.[2] Being forced into poverty because of his efforts to pay off his father's debts, Henry Percy would eventually become known as 'The Unthrifty Earl', although probably not in his own lifetime. Moreover, the ill feeling that existed between Percy and his brothers was such that he nominated King Henry as his heir in preference to them. In the same way, Cavendish attributed Wolsey's downfall to a grudge nurtured by Anne in the aftermath of the breaking of her betrothal to Henry Percy.

Either way, it is too simplistic to attribute Wolsey's downfall solely to the machinations of Anne Boleyn. Indeed, while King Henry sought to obtain the annulment of his marriage to Katherine it was desirable to keep the cardinal on side. Anne was very much

1. Allington Castle, Kent. The home of Thomas Wyatt.

2. Alnwick Castle, Northumberland. Henry Percy's primary residence as Earl of Northumberland.

3. Anne Boleyn from the portrait held at Hever Castle. The rival of Venus.

ANNA BOLLINA   VXOR HEN V

4. Anne Boleyn from the portrait held at Ripon Cathedral and recently heralded as likely to be the closest depiction of Anne.

Above right:
5. Autograph of Henry
Percy, sixth Earl of
Northumberland.

Above left: 6. Anne
Boleyn from the portrait
held in the Royal
Collection.

Left: 7. Anne Boleyn
as depicted in historical
fiction.

Opposite: 8. Anne by
Hans Holbein.

Above: 9. Typical dress of a Tudor lady in waiting by Hans Holbein.

Left: 10. Device of Queen Claude. François I's Queen; Anne served as a maid of honour in her household; her court is often thought to have been too dull for the high-spirited Anne.

11. Hever Castle, Kent. Anne Boleyn's family home was the probable setting for a scandalous story of Anne Boleyn and Thomas Wyatt.

Above, below and opposite top: 12, 13 & 14. Greenwich. The setting for the gorgeous pageant, the Castle of Loyalty. Many jousts were held here, including the one on the fatal May Day of 1536.

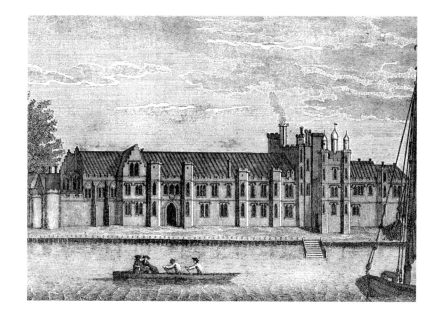

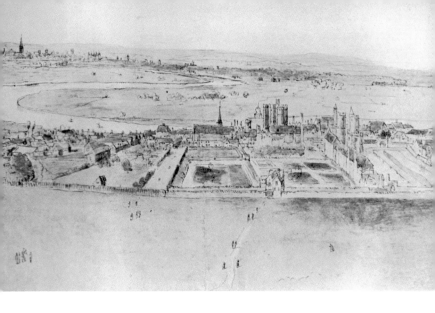

15. Henry Percy,
sixth Earl of
Northumberland.
Probably Anne
Boleyn's first
love; their desire
to marry was
thwarted by
Henry VIII and
Cardinal Wolsey.

Above left: 16. Henry VIII. Henry's interest in Anne forced Thomas Wyatt to step aside.

Above right: 17. Margaret of Austria, Regent of the Netherlands. Anne was educated at Margaret's court, where she acquired much of her refinement. Margaret was shamelessly courted by Charles Brandon, an event possibly witnessed by Anne.

Left: 18. Mary Tudor, the French Queen and Charles Brandon, Duke of Suffolk. Anne was briefly maid of honour to Mary. Upon the death of Louis XII, Mary manipulated Suffolk into marrying her. Suffolk and Thomas Wyatt later became enemies and it is highly probable that Wyatt's imprisonment in the Tower was due to an altercation between the two men.

19. Mary Tudor, the French Queen. Anne and Mary did not get on; perhaps Anne was disapproving of Mary's behaviour in France.

20. Thomas Boleyn. Anne Boleyn's father appeared to prefer his daughter's alliance with Henry Percy, rather than James Butler.

21. Henry VIII by Hans Holbein.

This page spread top: 23. London Bridge *c.*1600.

24 & 25. *Above:* Westminster *c.*1550. *Below:* Westminster Hall. Anne's alleged accomplices, Sir Henry Norris, Sir Francis Weston, William Brereton and Mark Smeaton were tried and condemned here.

Above: 26. London as Anne Boleyn would have known it.

Below: 27. The Tower of London. Anne Boleyn was imprisoned here in May 1536, as was Thomas Wyatt. The poet witnessed the executions of Anne's alleged accomplices, a scene that changed his life forever. Anne was tried in the White Tower; among her judges was her former suitor, the Earl of Northumberland.

Above left: 28. James Butler. Negotiations for the marriage of Anne and James began while she was still in France. When neither family could reach agreement, the match was abandoned.

Above right: 29. Thomas Wyatt. The romantic poet is believed to have courted Anne. However, the fact that he was already married meant that their love could not go far.

Above left: 30. Thomas Cromwell. Cromwell played a large part in the fall of Anne Boleyn. However, a friend to Thomas Wyatt, he interceded on the poet's behalf after the fall of Anne.

Above right: 31. Cardinal Thomas Wolsey. Wolsey was arrested by Henry Percy, sixth Earl of Northumberland. The earl had been a page in Wolsey's household as a youth and he had been censured over his relationship with Anne Boleyn.

aware of this. Relations between Wolsey and the future Queen were even cordial at times, especially considering the stress that all parties must have been under as one obstruction after another caused the affair to drag on for the best part of six years.

Evidence for the geniality that existed between Anne and Wolsey can be seen in letters written to the cardinal by Anne, such as the one written while both were recovering from the dreadful sweating sickness that swept the country in the summer of 1528:

> My Lord, in my most humblest wise that my poor heart can think I do thank your grace for your kind letter, and for your rich and goodly present, the which I shall never be able to deserve without your great help, of the which I have hitherto had so great plenty that all the days of my life I am most bound of all creatures next the king's grace to love and serve your grace, of the which I beseech you never to doubt that ever I shall vary from this thought as long as any breath is in my body.[3]

It was necessary, in the early stages at least, for Anne and Wolsey to become allies. Anne, if she were to marry Henry, needed Wolsey's help. Equally, Wolsey, now that he knew that his master was determined to marry Anne, understood that supporting him was the only way to continue in royal favour. It was, therefore, a marriage of convenience, although it was not to last.

The reasons given by Ambassador Mendoza for Anne's grudge are entirely plausible. It was certainly true that Wolsey, fearing the rise of the Boleyns, had prevented Sir Thomas's promotion to the post of comptroller of the household in 1519, although it was but a temporary postponement. Also, when Wolsey knew of Henry's desire to put aside Queen Katherine, he had set about negotiating a match for the King with a foreign princess; certainly a French candidate, as Mendoza had suggested, had not been ruled out.

It was only at the turn of 1530, seven years after the breaking of her affair with Henry Percy, that Anne decided the cardinal was not acting in her own best interests. By then, of course, her enmity was not in connection with her union with Henry Percy, but with Henry VIII. It was at this point that she joined the ranks of those who had dedicated themselves to secure the cardinal's ruin. Once Anne had turned against Wolsey there was no going back. She worked tirelessly to ensure that any attempt on the part of the King to restore him to favour was successfully thwarted.

Nevertheless, Anne had a fight on her hands. For some time, Henry had been showing signs that he wished to restore the disgraced cardinal. Wolsey, upon being sent away, found himself in a lonely house without beds, sheets or furniture of any kind. Although there was more than enough food and drink for himself and his household, Wolsey was obliged to borrow plates, dishes and linen.

His circumstances had not improved when, on a rainy night at the beginning of November, he received a visit from Sir John Russell. The visit was as secret as it was unexpected, although it was authenticated by the gift of a ring from King Henry. Russell urged Wolsey to be of good cheer, for the King 'loveth you as well as ever he did and is not a little disquieted for your troubles'.

Shortly after this, Wolsey was given all the household items he needed, although some oversight on the part of the officers meant that it was not as abundant as the King has wished.[4]

Perhaps the ambassador, Jean du Bellay, was right after all when he speculated that 'it is probable that he [Wolsey] will regain his authority'.[5] However, du Bellay had reckoned without the Dukes of Norfolk, Suffolk and Lord Rochford, Anne's father. Ambassador Mendoza had been more perceptive. Two years previously, he had seen which way the wind was blowing for the cardinal and had speculated that Wolsey was too powerful and able to be allowed to live in retirement or even in disgrace. Now, at the close of 1529, Norfolk, Suffolk and Rochford appeared to share this view. Cavendish speaks of them devising a means to 'disquiet and disturb his [Wolsey's] patience; thinking thereby to give him an occasion to fret and chafe, that death should rather ensue than increase of health or life, which they most desired'.[6]

Anne's feelings toward Wolsey are, at this stage, still somewhat ambiguous. It cannot be said for certain if, at this precise point, she was quite so eager to bring down Wolsey. At Christmas 1529, Wolsey fell ill and it was believed that he would die. Once again, Henry showed compassion to his former servant and sent his personal physician, Dr Buttes, to attend him. Dr Buttes visited the patient and returned to Henry to give his diagnosis. Without comfort from the King and Mistress Anne, he said, Wolsey would be dead within four days. The King was horrified, 'God forbid that he should die', was his reaction.

Henry then sent Dr Buttes back to Wolsey, urging him to do all he could to save him. Dr Buttes said that he would carry out the

King's wishes but, in order to save Wolsey, he had to take his some 'comfortable message' from the King. Henry's comfortable message took the form of a ring, the ruby of which was engraved with an image of his face. Henry then turned to Anne and asked her also to send a token with some comfortable words. Then, as Cavendish puts it, Anne 'being not minded to disobey the King's earnest request, whatsoever she intended in her heart towards the cardinal', took a gold tablet from her girdle and handed it to Dr Buttes 'with very gentle and comfortable words and commendations to the cardinal'.[7]

If, as Cavendish proposes, Anne had indeed been acting only in conformity with the King's will, it was not very long before she revealed her true feelings. For, once Wolsey had recovered his health, he was anxious to recover his position also. One person he knew he had to win over was Anne herself. However, Anne rejected the hand of friendship Wolsey extended to her. Ambassador Chapuys thought he could see through her as he wrote of a mission to reinstate the cardinal to favour. He noted that, 'but for the lady [Anne], this would be easy, for it is thought the King has no ill-will to the Cardinal'. Further on, he expresses his belief that Anne showed kindness towards Wolsey during his recent illness only because '[s]he must have thought he was dying, or shown her dissimulation and love of intrigue, of which she is an accomplished mistress'.[8] Chapuys, although obviously biased against Anne, was no doubt correct in his estimation of her in this instance. Anne did now turn against Wolsey. Then, in order to secure his downfall, she chose a method that would reunite her with someone from her past.

8

Henry Percy & the Arrest of Cardinal Wolsey 1530

Henry Percy and Anne Boleyn had parted in 1523. Despite the distrust in his father on the part of the King and the cardinal, the young Lord Percy had shown himself to be highly capable, and he had been made a member of the council of the north in 1522. Later that year, he became deputy warden of the east march. The warden-general, Thomas, second Baron Dacre, recognized the young man's potential and promoted him as a possible successor in the east, although without success. However, in the face of a possible war with Scotland that same year, Percy and his father were selected to advise the King's lieutenant-general, the Earl of Shrewsbury, Percy's future father-in-law.

Henry Percy's life up until now had been one of hope unfulfilled. Upon his leaving Wolsey's service, his betrothal to Mary Talbot had been revived and, some point between March 1525 and September 1526, they had married. The couple were very unhappy together and it looked as though no heir would be produced.

Percy's fortunes improved upon the death of his father in 1527, when he became the sixth Earl of Northumberland. Later that year, he was appointed warden of the east and middle marches towards Scotland. One of his first cases concerned Sir William Lisle of Felton,[1] constable of Alnwick Castle and a man of violence, whose actions against his neighbours had led to his imprisonment at York. Lisle escaped custody and had embarked on a series of raids on the properties of his opponents; even those in Cardinal Wolsey's lordship of Hexham were not safe. Upon Northumberland's appointment as warden, however, Lisle surrendered to him at Alnwick. Despite his best efforts, Northumberland was unable to save Lisle and the rebel was executed shortly afterwards. Notwithstanding this early failure, Northumberland was to become a trusted and respected figure in the north.

Northumberland's duties as a peer also brought him to Westminster from time to time. On one occasion, in 1529, he had acted as a trier of petitions in parliament. More recently, he was one of the many who had attended the council session held following the resignation of Wolsey as chancellor.

It is in connection with Cardinal Wolsey that Henry Percy was once again brought into the sphere of Anne Boleyn. It has often been said that Northumberland took up the charge to arrest Wolsey with the greatest of pleasure. However, if Cavendish's account[2] is to be believed, the experience was both daunting and discomforting to the earl.

According to Cavendish, Northumberland, accompanied by Walter Walsh, a gentleman of the privy chamber, and several of

Northumberland's retainers, arrived at Cawood Castle, near York one evening. Their first task was to get past the gate-keeper, who refused to give up the keys. So firm was he that Northumberland and Walsh were forced to agree to allow him to keep the keys provided he swore on the Bible not to let anyone in or out except on the earl's orders. This, surprisingly, the man did.

Wolsey, sitting at dinner, was tucking into his fruit when word came of Northumberland's arrival. At first Wolsey did not believe the news and he sent a servant to check. Upon hearing that his former page was waiting in the hall, Wolsey observed that there was nothing on the table for them to eat, but he sent a servant to see if anything could be brought for them. With that, he went to the hall to meet his unexpected guests.

Wolsey greeted Northumberland cordially. He told Northumberland that he had long wished to receive him as a guest in his home, adding that he ought to have given notice of his visit so that greater honour might have been paid him. Wolsey then offered him a bed for the night, suggesting that the earl might change his clothes in his own chamber while one was being prepared for him.

Still, Wolsey could not resist aiming a barb at the young man who had once been his servant, probably with the intent of demeaning him in front of his men. 'Ah, my lord', he began,

I perceive well that you have observed my old precepts and instructions which I gave you, when you were abiding with me in your youth, which was, to cherish your father's old servants, whereof I see here present with you a great number. Surely, my lord, ye do therein very well and nobly, and like a wise gentleman. For these be they that will not only serve and love you, but they will also live and die with you, and be true and faithful servants to you, and glad to see you prosper in honour; the which I beseech God to send you, with long life.

Wolsey, then, could not resist mocking the Earl of Northumberland. He not only compared him unfavourably with others who now held the station that had once been his, he also implied that Northumberland was guilty of disloyalty, suspecting, perhaps, that Northumberland's visit did not bode well for himself.

Having publicly derided the earl, Wolsey took him by the hand and led him into his chamber. With Cavendish standing at the door, the two men went to the window to talk. The cardinal's tactics might have confounded Northumberland and, according to Cavendish, he did appear somewhat shaken. Placing a hand on Wolsey's arm, and in a voice that was faint and soft, he said, 'My lord, I arrest you of high treason.'

Now it was Wolsey's turn to be confounded. Cavendish notes that his master stood still and silent for a long while. When he did speak, it was to ask Northumberland by what authority he arrested him. Northumberland replied that he was acting under a commission. Wolsey asked to see the commission, which request Northumberland refused. Wolsey then told Northumberland that he would not obey his arrest, putting it down to an ancient grudge that had existed between Wolsey and the earl's family.

As this was going on, Northumberland's companion, Walter Walsh, was in the process of arresting one of Wolsey's house-guests, Dr Augustine. Wolsey went up to Walsh and explained that, since Northumberland would not show him his commission, he would not yield himself to him. He continued, pointing out that Walsh was a gentleman of the privy chamber and as such had the power, at the King's command, to arrest the greatest peer of the realm even without a commission. Wolsey then surrendered to Walsh.

In spite of the treatment meted out to him, Northumberland continued to treat Wolsey with the utmost leniency and respect. Although Wolsey had a large guard, and Northumberland's men were fearful that they might rise up on their master's behalf, the earl allowed them to remain and wait upon and guard the cardinal. Northumberland allowed Wolsey to make his public farewells, complete with blessings, to his tenants and friends. That Sunday, he was allowed to celebrate mass in a private chapel at Cawood, following which he was transferred to the care of Sir Robert Lascelles, who escorted him to the Earl of Shrewsbury. Upon arrival at Shrewsbury's residence, Wolsey became ill and had to remain for several weeks. Despite having sufficiently recovered to travel once more, Wolsey's strength again failed him and he was forced to stop at Leicester. This was the end of his journey, for not long afterwards, he died.

Even in his darkest hour Wolsey refused take Northumberland seriously. He mocked him in front of his men as he had mocked and chided him in front of his fellow servants as a youth. Yet, throughout all this, Northumberland had retained his composure and discharged his duty in a respectful and professional manner.

Anne had exacted her revenge on Wolsey and she had used her former suitor as her agent. While no one celebrated the demise of Cardinal Wolsey more vigorously than the Boleyns, it can only be guessed what Northumberland's personal thoughts were with regard to his final dealings with his former master. Perhaps, as history accepts, he did take a secret pleasure in arresting him, seeing it as a way to avenge the ill-treatment he had received at his hands while a young page and the breaking up of his romance with Anne Boleyn. On the other hand, given his rough-handling by Wolsey, for Wolsey did not know when to stop even when he was on the canvas, it could be that Northumberland was sickened by the whole affair. Perhaps he even blamed Anne for placing him in such a difficult and unpleasant situation. The truth shall never be known.

9

The Pre-Contract 1532

The arrest of Cardinal Wolsey was not the last time Henry Percy would cross the path of Anne Boleyn. The summer of 1532 brought Henry VIII to a crisis point in his attempt to subdue clerical opposition to the annulment of his marriage to Queen Katherine and the acceptance of his proposed marriage to Anne Boleyn. At this point, the spectre of Anne's previous relationship with Henry Percy returned, confronting the King with a new problem.

Even as his relationship with Anne was in the process of being broken, Lord Percy had told Wolsey that he and Anne had promised to marry. He seemed to imply that they had entered into a pre-contract, which, if consummated, could not have been broken by King or Pope. The fact that Percy later married Mary Talbot, albeit after a delay, suggests that the pre-contract had indeed been successfully resolved, the interval between their betrothal and marriage being caused by negotiations and legalities. Then, when Henry VIII applied to the Pope for a dispensation to marry Anne he noted the pre-contract, adding that it was null and void. However, subsequent events would show that Henry, despite his assurances and his optimism, was seriously mistaken in his belief that the matter of the pre-contract had been settled.

It was widely known that the Earl and Countess of Northumberland failed to get on. In truth, their marriage was a disaster. Their neighbours in the north blamed the couple's marital woes on Percy's churlishness. The truth of the matter was, quite simply, that Lord Percy and his wife hated each other and had done so from the moment they had set eyes on each other. Indeed, the marriage seemed doomed even before it had begun. The wedding itself had been a miserable, meagre affair. In contrast to other Percy weddings, no largesse was distributed and 'the poor were sent hungry from the gates'.[1] Even so, that was just the beginning.

The couple were forced to live in relative poverty. Their situation was due to a combination of the rigid economy imposed upon them by Percy's father, as well as Cardinal Wolsey's constant interference in the life of his former page, which included the placing of servants into the Percy household to act as spies. Percy mentioned his harsh treatment in a letter to Thomas Arundel, in which he states that 'neither by the king nor by my lord cardinal am I regarded'.[2]

Matters did not improve following the death of the old Earl of Northumberland. Debts inherited by Henry Percy, now the sixth earl, did little to enhance the couple's financial prospects. They lived on a weekly sum of six shillings and ten pence each.[3] From this allowance the new earl and countess had to pay for all their meat and drink. Their servants – two male and two female attendants were allowed them – were paid a wage of one shilling and sixpence a week. The countess's wardrobe was valued at a mere £40, including her jewellery. As though this were not bad enough, the Countess Mary was said to be cold and unsympathetic. Insensitive to her husband's delicate state of health, she took every opportunity to pick quarrels with him and to plot with her family against him.

Given the circumstances under which they lived, it must have come as a great surprise to everyone to learn that the couple were to become parents. Even here, however, tragedy awaited them. Although almost full-term, the Countess Mary, taking advantage of the fact that her husband was away on business, left the family home and rode in stages to one of her father's residences. As a result, in April 1529, she gave birth to a stillborn child. Mary fell seriously ill.

The first Earl Henry knew of the danger his wife now faced was when he received news from his father-in-law. Percy wrote to his friend, William Arundel:

> So it is that my wife is brought to bed of a child, and as I have word from my Lord Steward [Shrewsbury] and them about her, she looks for non other but death, and if she escape the physicians write plain she cannot continue.[4]

Yet, continue she did. Countess Mary recovered and, possibly at Wolsey's insistence, she returned to her husband. Nevertheless, relations between husband and wife did not improve. The main reason, apart from those differences in personality that caused the couple to jar, as well as the unwelcome and intimidating shadow of Cardinal Wolsey, was the constant interference by Mary's relatives. Her sister, Elizabeth, especially took advantage of the instability of the Percy marriage, telling tales about Northumberland, pointing out his failings and resurrecting his earlier relationship with Anne Boleyn. The ensuing quarrels proved too much and the couple eventually parted for good.

On the other hand, although several years had passed since their youthful romance, it seems that Anne Boleyn was never really far from Henry Percy's thoughts. During their many arguments, Earl Henry was supposed to have told his wife that he had loved Anne and had always regretted not marrying her. It is sometimes thought,[5] that Percy went so far as to tell his wife that he was not really her husband because, long ago, he and Anne had been pre-contracted to each other. The Northumberland marriage was, therefore, illegal. Countess Mary, far from being outraged, immediately understood that here was the key that would release her from her disastrous union. She wrote down what her husband had told her and sent it in a letter to her father, who passed it on to Anne's uncle, the Duke of Norfolk.

In another version,[6] the story of the pre-contract came about when the Earl of Shrewsbury had made it his business to prevent Anne's marrying King Henry and becoming Queen. Certainly, his views on the proposed marriage would not have been entirely unexpected. The Earl of Shrewsbury was a firm supporter of Queen Katherine. By default, he had no love for Anne Boleyn. Ambassador Chapuys reported, in March 1531, Shrewsbury's assertion that he would not hold the crown at Anne's coronation, even though it would be his duty to do so, adding for good measure that he would 'take care not to fall into dishonour by placing it on any other head but that of the present Queen'.[7] In fact Chapuys, who was not entirely conversant with English royal ceremonial, got things slightly wrong. It was Shrewsbury's duty to carry the sceptre, not the crown. Even so, when the time came, Shrewsbury did not attend the coronation, sending his son, Lord Talbot, in his stead.

In seeking the means to achieve his goal, Shrewsbury found the perfect solution in a story told to him by his daughter. According to Countess Mary, Northumberland had told her during a quarrel that he had loved Anne Boleyn and had wanted to make her his wife. Although no pre-contract is mentioned in this version, Percy's words were twisted into false charges against Northumberland, to which an actual pre-contract between Northumberland and Anne was added. This tale of woe was written into a letter, which was then handed to the Duke of Norfolk.

However it came about, it seems that Northumberland, in a fit of anger, had reminded the countess of his earlier love for Anne Boleyn, perhaps expressing his regret that he had not married her. Countess Mary, eager for any opportunity to injure her husband, had chosen to interpret his remarks as an admission of a previous marriage which was, as far as her husband was concerned, an act of bigamy.

It was clear that the problem of the pre-contract would not go away. It now represented a threat, not only to the Northumberland marriage, but also to that between Anne Boleyn and Henry VIII. It was necessary to proceed with all caution.

The Duke of Norfolk, in common with all concerned, had thought the problem had been laid to rest. He, like Shrewsbury, felt disinclined to approach King Henry directly about it. He did not want to risk incurring Henry's formidable wrath, not to mention that of Anne, should uncertainties about the pre-contract prove to be unfounded. Norfolk, therefore, thought the best course of action was to show the letter to his niece. Anne's response was typically audacious. She took the letter and placed it into the King's hands, insisting that a proper investigation should be made.

The Earl of Northumberland was rigorously examined on oath by the Archbishops of Canterbury and York. He swore that no pre-contract had ever existed between him and Anne. He then went before the Duke of Norfolk and others of the King's council and, swearing upon the blessed sacrament, firmly reiterated that there had been no pre-contract. For her part, Anne also swore that the two of them had not entered into any agreement to marry. With all parties satisfied, the matter was once again laid to rest, at least for the time being.

Percy's denial of a pre-contract between him and Anne Boleyn appears to contradict Cavendish's assertion that he and Anne had agreed to marry. However, as previously noted, it could simply be a question of consummation. Perhaps the young lovers had pledged to marry, but, unless they had gone on to consummate their relationship, their promise was not binding and could be broken. In this case, there really was no pre-contract to speak of. Thus, Northumberland told the truth when he denied its existence, as did Anne. On the other hand, had they pledged to marry and consummated their union, then, even without the benefit of a church ceremony, the couple were married in the eyes of man and God and their union was indissoluble.

The ambiguity surrounding the case certainly explains the delay in Percy's marriage to Mary Talbot, as has been shown. The fact that their wedding had gone ahead is a strong indication that the problems presented by the pre-contract had been satisfactorily resolved. It had not been an impediment to the Percy marriage; it would have no bearing on the union between King Henry and Anne Boleyn, at this stage, at least.

10

'Some Tyme I Fled' 1532–1533

On 10 May 1530, the imperial ambassador, Eustache Chapuys, reported a tit-bit of court gossip to his master. He mentioned that the Duke of Suffolk had been allowed to return to court following a period of exile. The duke's offence had been to denounce to Henry a criminal connection between Anne Boleyn and a gentleman of the court. The gentleman had already been dismissed from the court on the same suspicion. Suffolk had been sent away at the request of Anne herself who had been angry with him.[1]

The man with whom Anne was said to have had a criminal connection is not named but is believed by many to have been Thomas Wyatt. As is known, Anne's would-be suitor had indeed left the court once he realized the King was interested in Anne. His journey to Italy in company with Sir John Russell had, however, been self-exile, rather than dismissal.

On the other hand, Wyatt's current fall from grace was probably less to do with his association with Anne Boleyn, but caused instead by a disagreement between him and Charles Brandon, Duke of Suffolk; as shall be seen, there was some degree of enmity between the duke and the poet, although the cause is not fully understood. If the story of Suffolk's rustication is true, and not simply another case of self-exile, it did not appear to have lasted long. Henry wanted to be surrounded by his friends, so Suffolk was very soon returned to favour.

In the autumn of 1532, Henry and Anne journeyed to Calais for a meeting with François I. It had long been Wolsey's ambition that a *rapprochement* should be reached between England and France, and he had worked tirelessly to achieve it. Alas, his death, at the close of 1530, meant that he would never see the crowning of his efforts. Still, it remained necessary to cultivate the support of King François. With the Emperor Charles threatening invasion in support of his aunt on the one hand, and papal pressure exerted on the Spanish cardinals and ambassadors on the other, France was the only ally upon whom Henry could rely. Without François' help, Henry would never be able to marry Anne and remain safe. The threat to his kingdom was all too real.

King François had already pledged his support to Henry, but Henry, in these uncertain times, needed reassurance. In view of this, a meeting was arranged between the two kings at Calais. Meanwhile, in order to give her the necessary status, Anne Boleyn, Henry's future queen and consort, was raised to the rank of Marquess of Pembroke in her own right in a lavish ceremony.

As the court left England for Calais they were joined by Thomas Wyatt, who wrote a few lines in commemoration. Yet, it was not Calais, nor the splendour and pageantry of the occasion that inspired the poet, but Anne, or rather, his feelings for her:

Sometime I fled the fire, that me so brent,
By sea, by land, by water, and by wind;
And now the coals I follow that be quent,
From Dover to Calais, with willing mind.
Lo, how desire is both forth sprung, and spent;
And he may see, that whilom was so blind,
And all his labour laughs he now to scorn,
Meashed in the briars, that erst was only torn.[2]

Thomas confides that, although he was once passionately in love with Anne, he had tried very hard not to give in to his feelings. This he had singularly failed to do and now he is left to lament the fact that he had made a fool of himself over her. For Thomas Wyatt, as for Henry VIII, Anne Boleyn was, at one time or another, a 'great folly'.

The meeting with François was a success. So much so that it was believed by many that Anne and Henry had married while awaiting a calming of the storm that had whipped up the waters of the Channel and kept the party at Calais longer than expected. Others merely assumed that Anne and Henry had, at last, consummated their relationship and left it at that.

Whatever the case, a royal wedding did take place on 25 January the following year. Anne and Henry married in the presence of her father, mother, brother and two unnamed witnesses.[3] Even so, Anne was already pregnant. Although no official announcement had yet been made, there were rumours circulating, which were picked up by the ever sharp Ambassador Chapuys. In a story related to the

Emperor Charles, Chapuys states that Anne had been unable to keep the news of her pregnancy to herself any longer. Seeing one of her favourite courtiers, usually accepted as having been Thomas Wyatt, Anne seized him and told him that three days ago she had felt such a craving to eat apples and that when she had mentioned it to the King he had said that it was a sign that she was with child, but that she had replied that it was not. Then she fell into a fit of laughter.[4]

Anne, however, was indeed pregnant. Her condition had become obvious to all by the time of her coronation, at which Thomas Wyatt served as chief ewerer, deputising for his father, Sir Henry.[5] Within three months, on 7 September 1533, Anne gave birth to her first child, a daughter named Elizabeth. At about this time a curious incident occurred which may or may not have had any direct connection with Thomas Wyatt. It is worth recording, nevertheless, because it involves a man who was living at the Wyatt home, possible as a chaplain to Sir Henry.

William Glover wrote to Queen Anne telling her that he had received a messenger of Christ, who had commanded him to take a message to Anne. Glover did not believe the messenger, thinking he was an emissary of the devil. On the third appearance, however, the messenger revealed himself to be an angel. Glover now agreed to do his bidding, which was to tell Anne that she 'should have been quene of Inglande these 10 yeres past'. Glover left the letter with John Averey, master of the King's flagons. When Anne did become Queen, Glover was bidden to leave things alone, yet he told Dr Bruton about the messenger. Then, following Anne's coronation, the messenger returned and bade Glover to tell Anne that she was with child. Glover was told that Anne was at Windsor and that the child was a girl 'whiche shulde be a princes [sic] of the land'. Glover told this to Dr Bruton also, adding that the Queen would give birth at Greenwich. Dr Bruton passed the message on to Anne's chaplain, Mr Gwynne, who visited Glover, bringing Anne's almoner with him. Mr Glover, however, was reluctant to repeat to them what the messenger had told him. Nevertheless, after three days, the messenger came once more and commanded Glover to write to Anne or else his master, Christ, would strike. Presumably, it was in order to escape the wrath of Christ that Glover finally committed his messages to paper, which he then sent to Anne. His letter was signed 'William Glover, dwelling with Sir Henry Wyatt'.[6]

What to make of Glover's curious testimony? It is difficult to speculate upon what he might have hoped to achieve by sending Anne news of something that was already known to her, namely, that she would have a daughter who, as could reasonably be expected at the time, would be a princess of the land. It is interesting that he should have told Anne that she should have been queen ten years earlier than she actually was. This would have meant that she should have worn the crown as early as 1523. At that time she was deeply involved with Henry Percy, then heir to the earldom of Northumberland. Had things gone as the couple had hoped they would, Anne would have become a countess, not a queen. Also, King Henry had probably not even noticed Anne at this stage. His heart had been taken by Mary Carey, née Boleyn, and she would not lose it for another three years yet.

11

All the Queen's Men: The Perils of Courtly Love, May 1536

One of the first things Anne Boleyn said upon her arrival at the Tower of London following her arrest was, 'O, Norris, hast thou accused me? Thou art in the Tower with me, and thou and I shall die together'.[1]

Norris is Henry Norris, groom of the stool and keeper of the privy purse. One of the most attractive and popular men at court, 'Gentle Mr Norris', as he was known, had become the royal favourite following the death of Sir William Compton in 1528. Born in the late 1490s, Norris was slightly younger than the King. His family had long been attached to royal service. His great-grandfather, Sir John Norris, had held the post of keeper of the great wardrobe under Henry VI. His grandfather, Sir William Norris, had been a knight of the body to Edward IV. Sir William was attainted following the rebellion led by the Duke of Buckingham against Richard III, whereupon he fled to Brittany. Here, he joined the entourage of Henry Tudor and it is possible that he fought on Henry's side at Bosworth. Certainly he had a command at Stoke in June 1487. From 1488, he had held the post of lieutenant of Windsor Castle. On his mother's side, Henry

Norris descended from the de Vere Earls of Oxford, who had also been the enemies of Richard III.

Henry Norris received his first royal grant in 1515. Two years later, he was serving in the privy chamber and was already beginning to establish a small entourage of his own. By 1518, he had begun to handle money on the King's behalf and was probably appointed as one of the newly designated gentlemen of the privy chamber in September of the same year.

Obviously in high favour, Norris was granted an annuity of fifty marks in January 1519. In May of that year, he survived Wolsey's weeding out of the King's minions in what might be seen as a forerunner to the purge under the Eltham ordinances that was to follow seven years later.

Henry Norris's loyalty was, clearly, not in doubt, but he had other qualities that made him attractive as a courtier too. He was an active participant in pageants and other festivities, such as the celebrations held in honour of the betrothal of the two-year-old Princess Mary to the even younger Dauphin of France in October 1518. To the King's delight, Norris excelled at the joust. It can be expected that his skills were put to good use as he accompanied the court to the Field of Cloth of Gold in 1520.

One of Norris's first tasks as groom of the stool and keeper of the privy purse was to look after the items, including jewellery, that had been presented to King Henry as New Year gifts.[2] Within two years Norris was appointed keeper of the manor of Placentia

(Greenwich) and of the great and little gardens there, as well as keeper of East Greenwich park and tower.[3]

Norris had married, some time prior to 1526, Mary, the daughter of Thomas Fiennes, eighth Baron Dacre. The couple had two sons and a daughter. Their first child, a daughter, named Mary, after her mother, would grow up to marry Sir George Carew, who would lose his life in 1545 as the captain of the unlucky *Mary Rose*. Their eldest son, also Henry Norris, was born in about 1525 and would receive a reformist education alongside Henry Carey, the son born to Mary Boleyn shortly after her relationship with Henry VIII had come to a close. The couple's second son, Edward, would die in infancy in 1529.

From time to time Henry Norris would be entrusted with matters of some delicacy. On one occasion he carried the King's secret communications to Wolsey following the fall of the cardinal. For the courtesy and respect he showed to the disgraced minister, Norris was rewarded with Wolsey's sincere thanks and the gift of a cross, inside which was a piece of the Holy Cross, the true cross of Christ, which the cardinal had always worn next to his skin. Norris accepted the gift which, no doubt, he treated as the precious relic it was.

Norris, who had been a widower since at least 1530, was a regular feature within the Boleyn circle. Indeed, he was courting a lady in Anne's household, a cousin to the Queen, Mistress Shelton. For some reason, he had not yet asked for her hand and his hesitation had aroused Anne's curiosity:

I asked him why he did not go through with his marriage, and he made ensure that he would tarry a time. Then I said, 'You look for dead men's shoes, for if ought came to the King but good, you would look to have me.' And he said if he should have any such thought he would his head were off. And then she said she could undo him if she would; and therewith they fell out.[4]

Once Anne had reflected on this incident she became concerned about the treasonous connotations of her words. She urged Norris to go to her almoner, John Skyp, to swear that she was a good woman.[5]

At about the same time, although the precise chronology is difficult to establish, the Scottish evangelical, Alexander Ales, had made a visit to Greenwich to seek authorization from Cromwell for a stipend awarded to him by the King. Much later, he recalled the event, and, addressing Queen Elizabeth, wrote:

Never shall I forget the sorrow which I felt when I saw the most serene Queen, your most religious mother, carrying you, still a little baby, in her arms and entreating the most serene King, your father, in Greenwich Palace, from the open window of which he was looking into the courtyard, when she brought you to him.

I did not perfectly understand what had been going on, but the faces and gestures of the speakers plainly showed that the King was angry, although he could conceal his anger wonderfully well. Yet from the protracted conference of the Council, (for whom the crowd was waiting until it was quite dark, expecting that they would return to London,) it was most obvious to everyone that some deep and difficult question was being discussed.

Nor was this opinion incorrect. Scarcely had we crossed the river Thames and reached London, when the cannon thundered out, by which we understood that some persons of high rank had been committed to prison within the Tower of London. For such is the custom when any of the nobility of the realm are conveyed to that fortress, which is commonly called the Tower of London, there to be imprisoned.[6]

Ales had witnessed the opening scene of the tragedy that was the fall of Anne Boleyn. Whether or not the King's anger had been in response to the altercation between Anne and Henry Norris is unclear. However, it would surely be to press coincidence a little too far to suggest that there was no connection between any of these events. What is known is that, upon the King's departure from the May Day joust, Norris was one of the six gentlemen chosen to accompany him. As they rode back towards Westminster, the King rigorously examined Norris,[7] asking him what he knew of Anne's sexual conduct; was she an adulteress; was Norris her lover? Norris steadfastly protested his innocence. Even when Henry offered him a full pardon if he told the truth, his long-standing and loyal friend could not lie to his King. Norris was dropped off at York Place, where he spent the night. The next day, at dawn, he was a prisoner of Sir William Kingston at the Tower.

According to Chapuys, writing the same day, Norris had been committed to the Tower because, while knowing about the Queen's adultery, he had not revealed the matter.[8] Anne, now held prisoner in the Tower, was also aware of what had brought her to the situation in which she now found herself. 'I am as clear from the company of men as for sin as I am clear from you,' she protested to William Kingston, 'and am the King's true wedded wife.'

Anne's fear was such that she, not unnaturally, wanted to know how other members of her family fared. Asked where her father was, Kingston replied that he had seen him before dinner at court. Anne then asked about her 'sweet brother', George. Kingston assured her that he had left him at York Place. Here, William Kingston was speaking the truth in the most literal sense; he had indeed last seen George Boleyn at York Place, but he neglected to tell Anne that her brother had since been brought to the Tower and had arrived few short hours after she had.

Anne was in a state of high anxiety. Sergeant[9] likens her to the distraught Ophelia, the tragic sister of Shakespeare's anti-hero, Hamlet. Anne's mood swung from serenity, asking for the sacrament to be brought to her chamber, to near hysterics, in which she babbled aimlessly, attempting to make sense of what was happening to her. In her ramblings she mentioned the name of Mark Smeaton: 'Mark, thou are here too.'

Biographical details for Mark Smeaton are difficult to find, probably because he was, as Anne herself described him, 'no gentleman'.[10] According to George Cavendish,[11] this 'unimportant' person was the son of a carpenter, a man who purchased his living with the sweat of his face. His mother supplemented the family income by spinning.

Possibly Flemish, and variously described as a singer, a dancer, a player on the virginals, the spinet or the lute, Smeaton is known to have been at court since at least 1529. The royal account books record payments for his shirts, hose, shoes and bonnets from this date. It is possible that he had been in the service of Cardinal Wolsey prior to this time, or was once a member of the Chapel Royal.

On 30 April, Smeaton was arrested and taken to Thomas Cromwell's house in Stepney, where he was vigorously interrogated. It has been speculated that he was also tortured. While Cromwell did not keep torture instruments in his house, George Constantine, a servant of Henry Norris,[12] had heard that Smeaton had been 'grievously racked', although he was unable to determine the truth of it. The *Chronicle of King Henry VIII of England*[13] speaks of Smeaton's having been held down by six men while a knotted rope was twisted about his head. On the other hand, Lancelot de Carles[14] specifically states that no torture was used. Whatever the case, Mark confessed to adultery with the Queen.

The *Chronicle of King Henry VIII of England* relates a tale wherein Smeaton was hidden in a closet by one of Anne's ladies. When Anne called for marmalade during the night, the lady would bring the musician, undressed and marmalade in hand, to her mistress. Once again we see echoes of the life of Katherine Howard. Also, this account reflects, albeit rather elaborately, contemporary gossip. How much of it applies to Anne Boleyn?

Later, Anne was told that Smeaton was the 'worst cherished' of any of the men in prison because he was held in irons. She offered that it was because he was no gentleman. She went on:

> but he was never in my chamber but at Winchester, and there she sent for him to play on the virginals, for there my lodging was above the King's... for I never spoke with him since but upon Saturday before May Day; and then I found him standing in the round window in my chamber of presence. And I asked why he was so sad [serious], and he answered and said that it was no matter, and then she said, You may not look to have me speak to you as I should do a noble man because you be an inferior person. No, no, madam, a look sufficed me, and thus fare you well.[15]

Mark had then walked away without waiting to be dismissed. He had been insolent, certainly, but it was hardly a case for arrest, and it was no foundation at all for a charge of adultery.

Anne also appeared to have feared Francis Weston, who had been taken to the Tower a few days afterwards. At court as a page by 1526, Weston was soon marked out by Henry as a fine sportsman. In high favour with his sovereign, he became a member of the privy chamber in 1533. In the same year, at Anne's coronation, he was made a Knight of the Bath.

Weston married, in May 1530, Anne, the daughter and heiress of Sir Christopher Pickering of Killington in Cumberland. Nevertheless, George Cavendish[16] could refer to him as 'Weston the wanton', who 'wantonly lived without fear or dread'. One lady upon whom Francis Weston had cast honeyed thoughts was the enchanting Mistress Shelton, she who would later become the object of Henry Norris's desires. Anne had rebuked the youthful favourite, saying that he loved the lady more than he did his wife. Weston answered that 'he loved one in her [Anne's] house better than them both'. Anne was curious. She asked who that might be, to which Weston replied that it was Anne herself.[17]

Yet, Weston did not come alone to the Tower. At some point he was joined by Sir Richard Page. Sir Richard, who was a prisoner by 8 May, had little, if any connection with Anne Boleyn. A courtier by 1516, he had become, in 1532, a member of one of the two groups of gentleman to serve in the privy chamber on a rotating timetable of six weeks at a time. Others in his group included Sir Nicholas Carew and Sir John Russell. Page's recent biographer[18] has speculated that it was rivalry between the three men, under cover of the general upheaval of the time, that had led to the arrest and imprisonment of Richard Page in May 1536. When Anne was told of Page's imprisonment, she had little to say about it.

Another man, Sir Francis Bryan, would be questioned by Thomas Cromwell and then released. Bryan, a gentleman of the privy chamber, whom Cromwell nicknamed the Vicar of Hell, was related to the Boleyns; his mother was half-sister to Lady Elizabeth Boleyn, mother to Anne. However, relations between him and his kin had cooled somewhat since he had argued with George Boleyn at the end of 1534. Bryan returned to court after a long absence but it was not long before he left again for his estates in Buckinghamshire. Bryan's estrangement from the Boleyns might have been his salvation, although Cromwell's intervention was probably also a major factor.

Anne was quite unconcerned about the plight of Weston, Page and Bryan. When she heard that they were also in the Tower she, according to William Kingston, 'made very good countenance'. It is possible that Anne half expected Weston to have been arrested. However, the downfall of yet another courtier is more difficult to explain.

William Brereton[19] was a gentleman of the privy chamber. He had been at court since at least 1521 and was a groom of the privy chamber by 1524. Brereton attached himself to Henry Norris and he might have been one of the unnamed persons who had witnessed Anne Boleyn's marriage to the King. He was certainly in King Henry's favour, having been awarded many grants, which led to his becoming the principal royal servant in the marches of north Wales. It was here that his heavy-handed approach might have led to his downfall.

Brereton was known to be ruthless, even rigging a trial in order to bring about the death of an enemy. Yet George Constantine, who was employed by Henry Norris and who had gone to school with William Brereton,[20] declared himself at a loss as to why Brereton should have been arrested. It has been speculated that he stood in the way of Cromwell's ambitions for Wales,[21] if so, it is a clear case of Cromwell's using the storm of the Queen's fall as a cover in the sweeping away of his own enemies.

Anne could probably understand, if not justify, the presence of Norris, Weston and Smeaton behind the walls of the Tower. In the cases of Page, Bryan and Brereton, it is not surprising that she should greet the news of their arrest with such indifference. There was very little, if anything, to tie them to her beyond their presence at court in the service of the King. Yet there is one man whose arrest must surely had provoked some reaction in Anne. For, within days of her own arrival at the Tower, Thomas Wyatt was brought to that formidable fortress as a prisoner.

'Myn Extreme Enemye': Thomas Wyatt, May 1536

Thomas Wyatt, as he himself declared, had fallen out of love with Anne Boleyn, but, since he remained a favourite with the King, his former liaison clearly had no detrimental effect on his career. In 1529, or earlier, he had been made Marshal of Calais. At about the same time he had been granted a licence to import 1,000 tons of Gascoigne wine or Toulouse wood. In June of the following year, he was reappointed Marshal of Calais, although the post subsequently fell into the care of Sir Edward Ryngley. Returning to England in November, it appears that Wyatt preferred the court of the King to the garrison town across the Channel. In 1532, Wyatt, who was already squire of the body by this time, was made Justice of the Peace in Essex.

Then, on 15 May 1534, Thomas Wyatt became embroiled in an affray with the serjeants of London during which one of the serjeants was killed. The incident earned him a spell in the notorious Fleet. His disgrace did not last long. A month later, he was granted, for life, the conduct and command of all men able for war in the seven hundreds of Kent, the parishes of Tinderden, Goudhurst, Staplehurst and the Isle of Oxney in Kent, with licence to have twenty men in his livery.[1]

Wyatt was appointed High Steward of the Abbey of Malling in 1535. It is probable that he was knighted on Easter Day that same year while, in July, he leased from the crown the estate of Aryngden Park in Yorkshire.

The paths of Thomas Wyatt and Anne must, of necessity, have crossed many times. Sir Thomas had duties to the King and was a popular figure at court. Anne, for her part, kept a lively, merry court, where she indulged her fondness for poetry, music, dancing, singing and the delights of courtly love. Anne had a serious side to her character as well. She was an eager advocate of religious reform and, as such, was an attractive figure, role-model or patroness to other, like-minded people, including Sir Thomas Wyatt himself. Anne, as her motto insisted, was 'the most happy', but all this was to come to an end during the May Day weekend of 1536. Despite the cooling of his former passion for Anne, Thomas Wyatt would not be able to escape the calamity that was to sweep the court.

As the story is told in the *Chronicle of King Henry VIII of England*, Thomas Wyatt attended the joust held on May Day, at which he performed better than anyone else:

> When the jousts were finished and they were disarming, the captain of the guard came and called Master Norris and Master Brereton, and said to them, 'The King calls for you.' So they went with him, and a boat being waiting they were carried off to the Tower without anyone hearing anything about it. Then Cromwell's nephew said

to Master Wyatt, 'Sir, the Secretary, my master, sends to beg you to favour him by going to speak with him, as he is rather unwell, and is in London. So Wyatt went with him.

It seems that the King sent Cromwell to tell him to have Wyatt fetched in order to examine him. When they arrived in London Cromwell took Master Wyatt apart, and said to him, 'Master Wyatt, you well know the great love I have always borne you, and I must tell you that it would cut me to the heart if you were guilty in the matter of which I wish to speak.' Then he told him all that had passed; and Master Wyatt was astounded, and replied with great spirit, 'Sir Secretary, by the faith I owe to God and my King and lord, I have no reason to distrust, for I have not wronged him even in thought. The King well knows what I told him before he was married.' Then Cromwell told him he would have to go to the Tower, but he would promise to stand by his friend, to which Wyatt answered, 'I will go willingly, for as I am stainless I have nothing to fear.' He went out with Richard Cromwell, and nobody suspected that he was a prisoner, and when he arrived at the Tower Richard said to the captain of the Tower, 'Sir Captain, Secretary Cromwell sends to beg you to do all honour to Master Wyatt.' So the captain put him into a chamber over the door...[2]

Quite what were the circumstances under which Thomas Wyatt was detained is not known and the account given in the Spanish *Chronicle* is probably as good as any other in this respect. Here, the poet is acquainted with the events that had taken place since the May Day joust: the arrest of Mark Smeaton, Henry Norris, William Brereton and Francis Weston, as well as that of George Boleyn and of the Queen herself in rapid succession.

The arrest of Thomas Wyatt at the fall of Anne Boleyn is often taken as the main cause of the rumours that later circulated within the Catholic sphere about the relationship between him and Anne. This, of course, proved inspirational to Harpsfield and Sander who, as has been shown, offered their own versions of the affair.

Still, Thomas Wyatt's previous association with Anne, as well as his well-earned reputation as an adulterer and *homme à femme*, were enough to almost guarantee his involvement, however slender, in the dreadful events that were to unfold.

In a letter, since badly damaged by fire, William Kingston writes to Cromwell noting that Anne gave little reaction when she was told that Wyatt was now a prisoner in the Tower. She appears even to have made a joke about his situation. Asking Lady Kingston whether the men had anyone to make their beds for them, she was told, 'Nay, I warrant you.' Then Anne said, 'They might make balettes well now,' punning on 'pallets' and 'ballets', 'but there is none but Rochford who can do it.' 'Yes,' rejoined Lady Kingston, 'Master Wyatt.' 'By my faith,' said Anne, 'thou hast said true.'[3]

If Anne was nonchalant about Wyatt's imprisonment, his father seems to have been even more so. A story, albeit unauthenticated, tells of how Sir Henry found out about his son's plight.[4] It was the dead of night and Sir Henry was awakened from his sleep by a messenger who handed him a letter. Having read it, the old knight said of his son: 'If he be a true man, as I trust he is, his truth will him deliver: it is no guile', whereupon he returned to his bed. Sir Henry slept the sleep of the innocent until the hour he was accustomed to awaken. He then set about writing the appropriate letters to the court after which he troubled himself no further.

If this story is unreliable as far as its details go, it does at least appear to capture the mood and the attitude of Sir Henry Wyatt at the time. On 7 May, he wrote a letter to his son. In it he explained that it was dangerous for him to ride out or to do his duty to the King at this time when his Grace has suffered by false traitors. He asked his son to give the King due attendance night and day: 'I pray to God to give him grace to be with him and about him that hath found out this matter, which hath been given him of God, and the false traitors to be punished according to the justice to the example of others.'[5]

At this stage, Sir Henry appears to be more concerned about the King than he is about his son's welfare. However, this was not the case. It soon becomes clear that he was in consultation with Thomas Cromwell, although it is uncertain which of the two men had initiated communications. Writing on 11 May, Sir Henry acknowledged a letter from Cromwell, which he had received the previous day. He thanked the secretary for the 'comfortable articles therein' touching his son, Thomas, and himself. He then ventured to ask when the King might see fit to free Thomas and show him 'that this punishment that he hath for this matter is more for the displeasure that he hath done to God otherwise,' and also to admonish him to fly vice and serve God better.[6] Sir Henry was worried about his son's moral conduct, which he understood to be a sin against God. Even now, however, he cannot have been entirely free of anxiety as those who shared his son's imprisonment were sent to trial.

Circa Regna Tonat, 12 May 1536

On 24 April 1536, two identical commissions of oyer and terminer had been appointed to investigate criminal activity, including unspecified treasons, in Middlesex and Kent. Those who sat included the chancellor, Sir Thomas Audley; Charles Brandon, Duke of Suffolk; Anne's uncle, the Duke of Norfolk; her father, Thomas Boleyn, now Earl of Wiltshire; and the chief secretary, Thomas Cromwell. Since the commissions were still active, they were now assigned the task of trying the alleged crimes of Queen Anne and her supposed accomplices.

In defiance of established practice, the commoners were tried first. In sessions held on Friday 12 May 1536, Sir Henry Norris, William Brereton, Sir Francis Weston and Mark Smeaton were brought before their judges. Mark Smeaton pleaded guilty of violation and carnal knowledge of the Queen, putting himself at the mercy of the King. Norris, Brereton and Weston asserted their innocence. The jury returned its verdict: all were guilty. The judgement against all four was that they were found guilty of treason and, as such, were sentenced to be executed at Tyburn.[1]

John Husee, the London agent of Lord Lisle, deputy of Calais, reported the news to his employer, noting that the four men had been arraigned and were 'judged to be drawn, hanged, and quartered. They shall die tomorrow or Monday'.[2] Husee was two days out in his estimation of when the men should die. Norris, Weston, Smeaton and Brereton were sent to their bloody and brutal deaths on Wednesday 17 May 1536, but what had really been their crime?

No documents relevant to the case survive. They might have been destroyed, perhaps in Queen Elizabeth's time; perhaps they had never existed at all. Therefore, the best account of the whole affair is provided by Ambassador Eustache Chapuys. In a typically lengthy letter to Charles V, written on 19 May, he noted that Mark Smeaton had 'confessed that he had been three times with the said *putain* [whore] and Concubine. The others were condemned upon presumption and certain indications without valid proof or confession'.[3] In other words, not even Chapuys, Anne's particular enemy, believed that the charges against the men were valid, or at least, he understood that they could not be proven.

It would seem that, in the final analysis, Sir Henry Norris and Sir Francis Weston, like Mark Smeaton, might have taken the game of courtly love beyond propriety. More probably, and this is more apparent in Norris's case, it was Anne who had acted and spoken inappropriately. No longer was the convention, in which the gentleman made love-sighs at his lady, being followed. Now it was the lady, Anne, who had reversed the role, spoken out of turn and had inadvertently placed herself and Norris in grave danger.

Whatever the truth of the matter, it is easy to understand how the exchange between the Queen and Norris could have been manipulated to imply an actual relationship between them. Indeed, this is exactly what did happen. By the time the formal allegations were made against her, Anne's words had been interpreted to suggest that there had been a promise between her and Norris to marry after the king's death, and that it seemed that they had hoped for this to happen.[4] The conduct and, perhaps more importantly, the conversation, of Norris, Weston and Smeaton, were such that it could easily have been misrepresented by those who would destroy the Queen.

As to Mark Smeaton, despite his ill-treatment following his detention, which could have been construed as the reason for his confession, thus invalidating it, he never retracted it. On the contrary, he consistently refused to deny the allegations against him and went to his death begging the crowd: 'Masters, I pray you all, pray for me, for I have deserved death.'[5]

It has been speculated[6] that Mark had become infatuated with Anne. Being a member, albeit on the fringes, of the flirtatious world of courtly love that marked the character of the Queen's household, he had, perhaps, come to believe that his love might be returned. Anne's reminding him, most pointedly, of the differences in their status and class quickly disabused him of this hope and, in his disappointment, he decided to exact his revenge on his mistress. Such, then, was the reason for his confession to having committed adultery with her. In a similar vein, perhaps Mark had not the wit to know that he was but a servant in the menial, not the chivalric sense.[7] It is important to observe, however, that Mark might have refused to retract his confession because, whatever his motives, he had been promised an easier and quicker death if he continued his stance.[8]

Yet, was there more behind this affair than innocent courtly love, the conventions of which had been misconstrued? The *Epistre contenant le Proces Criminel faite a l'encontre de la Royne Anne Boullant d'Angleterre* is a history written in verse by Lancelot de Carles and completed on 2 June 1536, only weeks after the events of which it speaks. De Carles was the almoner to the Dauphin and, at the time he composed his poem, was acting as secretary to the French ambassador, Antoine de Castlenau, Bishop of Tarbes. In time, de Carles would become Bishop of Reiz. Where it is possible to compare the information given in the poem with other contemporary documents, it is found to be accurate.

According to de Carles, Smeaton's arrest followed accusations made against him, Sir Henry Norris and George Boleyn by the sister of one of King Henry's courtiers. This courtier, since plausibly identified as Anthony Browne, had reproached his sister, Elizabeth Browne, Lady Worcester, for her apparently immoral behaviour. Since she was pregnant at the time, it is possible that her brother was implying that the baby was not her husband's, but that of a lover. In her defence, Lady Worcester suggested that if her brother thought her own behaviour bad, he should look to the Queen, who was sleeping with Mark Smeaton, Henry Norris and even her own brother, George.

Certainly Anne had a reputation, in certain circles at least, for immorality. As early as 1532, she was being spoken of as a 'common stewed whore',[9] or a 'whore and a harlot'.[10] Then, of course, there was her own uncle, the Duke of Norfolk, who called Anne 'a great prostitute'.[11]

It is possible that such slurs on Anne's character were inspired by sympathy for Queen Katherine. A certain Mistress Amadas had said that 'Anne should be burned, for she is a whore', adding, interestingly, that Henry Norris 'was bawd between the King and her'.[12] Mistress Amadas was the wife of Robert Amadas, master of the King's jewel house. She might once have been Henry's mistress prior to his relationship with Mary Boleyn. Since that time, however, she had been discarded by her husband. As such, her sympathies lay firmly with other wronged wives, such as the Duchess of Norfolk and, particularly, Queen Katherine. Similarly, Thomas Jackson, a chantry priest, had asserted that the King was living in adultery with Anne before his marriage and after.[13]

Perhaps the most damning 'evidence' of Anne's supposedly loose morals comes from a member of her own household. In the words of her vice chamberlain:

> as for pastime in the queen's chamber, [there] was never more. If any of you that be now departed have any ladies that they thought favoured you, and somewhat would mourn at parting of their servants, I can no whit perceive the same by their dancing and pastime they do use here.[14]

This gaiety has nothing to do with what was said, no intrigues conducted in window embrasures, no rebukes to courtiers who showed themselves reluctant to marry or who foolishly confessed their love for her. Rather, Anne, whose coronation had taken place only days earlier, was still celebrating with her ladies. Her court would, of course, continue to be one where dancing and pleasure was a regular feature. In this, it very much reflected the happy court she had known in her youth, when she had served the Archduchess Margaret.

Certainly love intrigues did have their place within Anne's household. Whether they can be extended to Anne and used as evidence of her alleged infidelity to the King is another matter. Her accusers felt they could make a case of them and they did.

The guilty verdicts against Norris, Weston, Brereton and Smeaton condemned Queen Anne by implication; if they were guilty, she was guilty. Anne herself had expected this to happen. Upon her arrival at the Tower she had asked of her gaoler, 'Mr Kingston, shall I die without justice? And I said, the poorest subject the King hath, hath justice. And there with she laughed.'[15]

John Husee informed Lord Lisle that Anne and Lord Rochford were due to be arraigned in the Tower, perhaps on Saturday or on Monday at latest. He speculated that they would suffer there immediately 'for divers considerations, which are not yet known'. He next speaks of Sir Richard Page and Sir Thomas Wyatt, noting that, although they were in the Tower, 'it is thought without danger of life, though Mr. Payge is banished the King's court for ever'.[16]

Notwithstanding Husee's optimism concerning Sir Thomas Wyatt, there were those who thought that he would not escape, but would share the same fate as the other men. Again, John Husee is our informant. His letter of Saturday 13 May states that: 'Here are so many tales I cannot tell what to write. This day, some say, young Weston shall escape, and some that none shall die but the Queen and her brother; others, that Wyatt and Mr. Payge are as like to suffer as the others...'[17]

Before such uncertainty could be resolved, however, Anne's predicament was to take an even more sorrowful turn. Although she was not yet aware of it, her marriage to Henry was to be annulled and her beloved daughter, Elizabeth, was to be declared illegitimate. This was necessary because Elizabeth, like Mary before her, now posed a threat to any child born to the King and his new wife of a legal marriage, Jane Seymour. Legitimacy was the key. It was imperative that the legitimacy of any child Henry had with Jane could be not be disputed. Henry must have a clean, fresh beginning. The man who was expected to help bring this about was the love of Anne's younger days, Henry Percy.

Persecuted Innocence,
13–16 May 1536

As early as December 1534, Henry Percy, sixth Earl of Northumberland had declared himself deeply offended by the insolence of the Boleyns and was ready to join the league against his former sweetheart.[1] This, at least, is what Eustache Chapuys had heard from Northumberland's physician, who was a client of the ambassador's.[2] The earl, the physician had said, was no longer such a friend of the King and of his ministers as he used to be, not least because he had been ill-treated by members of the government and had declared that those who had behaved this way towards him would soon have cause to repent of their ill-doings.

Northumberland, Chapuys' report continued, was particularly offended by Anne Boleyn, who was acting with arrogance and wickedness. On one occasion, she had 'heaped more injuries on the Duke of Norfolk than on a dog' to the point that the duke had felt obliged to leave the royal chamber. Outside, Norfolk encountered a gentleman he no longer regarded as a friend; even so, his anger caused him to forget whom he was addressing and he began to complain bitterly about his niece, referring to her, among other things as a 'great prostitute'.

Nevertheless, Anne's enemies, who would normally have turned such a state of affairs to their own advantage, were somewhat suspicious of the Earl of Northumberland. They considered him to be 'light and hasty', and warned Chapuys to be cautious in his dealings with him.[3] Chapuys was right to heed their advice. There really is nothing to allow us to think that the Earl of Northumberland had become Anne's enemy. Apart from anything else, he had no reason to be.

At the time of Anne's arrest, Northumberland was staying at one of his houses at Newington Green. He could not have been unacquainted with the enfolding events at the court. What he thought or understood about them cannot be known. Surely he must have heard the news about the new woman in King Henry's life, Jane Seymour. He might even have been aware that Jane was not to be just another royal mistress after all, but that the King's feelings for her ran deeper than mere infatuation. His heart must have sunk as he considered how happy life could have been had he and Anne married. Certainly, he would not have been forced to endure the sorrow of a failed marriage; Anne would not now be facing the indignity and grief of a discarded wife.

As it was, it can be speculated that Northumberland, like many who were not in Cromwell's confidence, thought that Anne would suffer no worse a fate than to be divorced from Henry. With history repeating itself, as it is wont to do, Anne would face a lonely future, as her predecessor, Queen Katherine, had done. The most obvious outcome was that Anne would be rusticated or sent to live abroad.

It was true that some effort had been made a few days previously to canvass theological opinion regarding a possible case for divorce. As early as 29 April, Ambassador Chapuys was able to write to his master with news that John Stokesley, Bishop of London, had been consulted about whether Henry could or could not abandon Anne Boleyn. Stokesley had wisely answered that he could give his opinion on such a matter only if the King himself asked for it. Even then, he added, he would try to 'ascertain what the King's intentions were, thereby implying, no doubt, that the King in his opinion could certainly desert his concubine, but that knowing the King's fickleness, he would not run the risk of offending her by proffering such advice'.[4]

At this stage, then, it is clear that the theological ground was being tested with a view to bringing the Boleyn marriage to an end. How much of this consultation process was known to the King can only be guessed. He could have initiated it. On the other hand, he might not even have been aware that the bishop had been approached. Whatever the case, a divorce was technically possible for two reasons. The first was Anne's previous pre-contract with Henry Percy. The second was Henry's previous relationship with Anne's sister, Mary.

By 2 May, as Anne was being conducted to the Tower, rumours once again began to circulate that Henry was seeking to divorce her on the grounds of her earlier relationship with Henry Percy: 'It is said that... the King had determined to leave her, as he had been informed that she had consummated a marriage with the earl of Nortemberlano (Northumberland) nine years ago.'[5]

Naturally, the ever-sharp Chapuys was also aware of the rumour, news of which he passed on to Charles V:

[t]his King, I have been for some days informed by good authority, had determined to abandon her; for there were witnesses testifying that a marriage passed nine years before had been made and fully consummated between her and the earl of Northumberland, and the King would have declared himself earlier, but that some one of his Council gave him to understand that he could not separate from the Concubine without tacitly confirming, not only the first marriage, but also, what he most fears, the authority of the Pope.[6]

In both cases the timing is incorrect. The relationship between Henry Percy and Anne Boleyn had ended by 1523. Notwithstanding this minor detail, the basic premise is sound. The pre-contract did provide King Henry with grounds to divorce Anne, but only if it could be upheld. For that, Northumberland's co-operation was essential.

The earl was approached by a friend, Sir Reynold Carnaby, who tried to persuade him to confess to a pre-contract. His answer was sent to Cromwell in a letter dated 13 May:

Mr Secretary, This shall be to signify unto you that I perceive by Sir Raynold Carnaby, that there is supposed a precontract between the queen and me; whereupon I was not only heretofore examined upon my oath before the Archbishops of Canterbury and York, but also received the blessed sacrament upon the same before the duke of Norfolk, and other the king's highness' council learned in the spiritual law; assuring you, Mr. Secretary, by the said oath, and blessed body which afore I received, and hereafter intend to receive, that the same may be to my damnation if ever there were any contract or promise of marriage between her and me. At Newington Green, the xiijth day May. In the 28th year of the reign of our sovereign lord, King Henry the VIIIth.[7]

Northumberland was insistent that no pre-contract had been entered into. That he swore on the holy sacrament, not once, but twice, is strong testament to the veracity of his statement; all the more so because Northumberland was very ill at the time and he did not expect to live much longer. He would not want to go to God with a lie on his lips. The earl's conscience was clear. Yet, while Northumberland might have been looking forward to the peace of death, life continued to show him nothing but cruelty.

Only two days after he had written his letter to Cromwell, he was called upon to attend the trial of his former sweetheart. Northumberland was, perhaps, the man least capable of fulfilling his responsibilities in this regard. By reason of compassion for his frail condition, and in view of his former attachment to Anne, Henry Percy, of all men, should have been excused this dreadful duty.

As early as April 1528, Northumberland had spoken of the return of his 'old disease and of a swelling of the stomach with extreme ague', adding that he expected shortly to die. He was ill again in late 1532, early 1533 and mid-1534. In February 1536 he wrote that he had not left his chamber at Topcliffe for a year because of his illness, although this statement fails to take into account a journey he had made to Newcastle the previous autumn. His illness obliged him to miss part of the Garter Feast of 1536. Now, as he prepared for the trial of Anne Boleyn, his infirmity could only worsen under the psychological stress the ordeal promised to heap upon him.

The nature of the earl's illness is unknown. It has been speculated[8] that the 'old disease' might have been a physical complaint or a psychological depression, assuming that the two could be distinguished in a man as chronically ill as Northumberland. Meanwhile, the ague caused him to shiver even on the hottest days. The Earl of Northumberland was in no condition to meet the challenges of his terrible duty.

The trial of Anne Boleyn and her brother, George, Viscount Rochford, was due to take place on 15 May. A good summary of it is given by Eustache Chapuys in a letter written to Charles V on 19 May.[9] The charges against Anne were: that she cohabited with her brother and other accomplices; that there had been a promise between her and Sir Henry Norris to marry after the King's death, a thing for which they had both hoped; Anne had given Norris certain medals, which Chapuys interpreted as evidence that Anne had poisoned the late Queen Katherine and was intriguing to do the same to the Princess Mary; Anne had also laughed at the King and the way he dressed, her attitude towards her husband making it clear that she did not love him, but was tired of him.

The charges against Anne, then, can be reduced to two factors: adultery and a lack of respect for the King. The second of these charges might have been entirely groundless, perhaps her behaviour best being seen as all of a piece with the stormy relationship Anne shared with Henry and upon which they both seemed to thrive. Her words, whatever they had really been, could have been taken out of context or misunderstood by other, more censorious, members of the court. However, when coupled with the first charge, that of adultery, they take on a more sinister quality.

Anne defended herself admirably, but it was to no avail. The verdict had been decided beforehand and the peers, including the Earl of Northumberland, were obliged to judge her guilty. Thus, Northumberland condemned Anne. The immense distress this caused him quickly took its toll. As he listened to the judgement that was passed upon Anne, to be burned or beheaded according to the King's pleasure, his strength finally failed him and had to be taken from the court. He was unable to continue at the trial of George Boleyn.[10]

Turning to Viscount Rochford, Ambassador Chapuys observed that he had been charged with cohabiting with Anne by presumption because he had once been found to have spent a long time with his sister. Also, Rochford disobeyed instructions relating to evidence provided by his wife. Anne had allegedly made disparaging remarks regarding the King's sexual ability. These remarks were written down and shown to Rochford at his trial. Although he was instructed not to read them out loud, he did so; this, according to Chapuys, it what ultimately sealed his fate. Finally, Rochford was also said to have spread rumours that called into question the paternity of Anne's daughter, Elizabeth. These were the official charges against George Boleyn. The truth was somewhat different.

George Boleyn's real 'crime' was to be Anne Boleyn's brother and Princess Elizabeth's uncle. He was intelligent and spirited enough to mount a powerful defence of his sister. He was powerful enough to provide the focus for Boleyn followers and, especially, those who would assert Elizabeth's rights as heir to the crown. George Boleyn, in other words, would fill a similar role to that of Charles V. He would become a thorn in the side of King Henry as he pressed for the rights of a daughter whom Henry had now come to regard as useless and, due to Henry's impending divorce of Anne, illegitimate. Rochford, therefore, had to be got out of the way. He was found guilty on the flimsiest of evidence and condemned to be drawn through the city of London to the gallows at Tyburn, where he was to be executed as a traitor.[11]

The following day, King Henry secured his divorce from Anne Boleyn. Notwithstanding Northumberland's denial, it was believed by some that the supposed pre-contract had indeed been used to annul the marriage of Henry VIII and Anne Boleyn. Charles Wriothesley[12] writes that a solemn court met at Lambeth, attended by the Archbishop of Canterbury, Thomas Cranmer, and the doctors of the law. At this court, it was declared that the marriage between Henry VIII and Anne Boleyn 'was, and always had been, utterly null and void, in consequence of certain and lawful impediments which, it was said, were unknown at the time of the union, but had lately been confessed to the Archbishop by the lady herself'.

Wriothesley thought that Anne's confession related to her pre-contract with Henry Percy, but this is not necessarily, the case. It has been pointed out[13] that the only confession needed from Anne was an oath confirming her blood relationship to Mary Boleyn. For, seeing, at last, that the Earl of Northumberland would not oblige the King by admitting to a pre-contract, other means were sought to secure the annulment of the marriage. This was found, as expected, in Henry's previous relationship with Anne's sister, Mary.

Ambassador Chapuys, who held a double doctorate in civil and canon law, understood this perfectly well. As he wrote to Charles V: 'The Archbishop had pronounced the marriage of the King and Concubine invalid on account of the King having had connection with her sister, and that, as both parties knew of this, the good faith of the parents cannot make the said bastard [Elizabeth] legitimate.'[14] Anne's marriage to King Henry had never really existed, and now this was acknowledged. The fact that this made a mockery of the charges of adultery against her did not seem to exercise Tudor minds overmuch.

'The Bell Towre Showed me Suche a Syght', 17 May 1536

On 17 May Thomas Wyatt stood by his window in the Bell Tower and witnessed a scene that would change his life forever. One after the other, George Boleyn, Viscount Rochford, whose sentence had been commuted to beheading, to take place on Tower Green; Sir Henry Norris; Sir Francis Weston; William Brereton and Mark Smeaton, were brought to the scaffold, its wooden floor strewn with straw that was quickly made slick with blood. The horror over, Wyatt, who was still uncertain of his own fate at this point, composed a poem in which he refers to 'these bloody days', which had broken his heart. The poem opens with a rubric, a Latin inscription in which Wyatt protests his innocence:

Innocentia

Veritas Viat Fides

Cicumdederunt me inimici mei

'For sure', he tells us, *circa Regna tonat* – about the throne the thunder rolls. Even then, however, the Bell Tower had not yet yielded all its horrors to Thomas Wyatt. On 19 May, John Husee wrote to Lady Lisle with news of the day's events: Queen Anne Boleyn had been executed. As to Wyatt and Page, they continued in the Tower. 'What shall become of them God knoweth best'.[1]

For Richard Page the ordeal was almost over. He was neither interrogated nor charged and, by 18 July, he was a free man. It is possible that Thomas Cromwell had intervened on his behalf.

Then, as May faded into June, the outcome for Thomas Wyatt began to look favourable indeed. On 11 June, Thomas Cromwell wrote to Sir Henry Wyatt with news of the King's pleasure, which was to release his son. Nevertheless, Cromwell urged Sir Henry to ensure that Thomas should 'address himself better than his wit can consider'. Sir Henry sent for Thomas and commanded him to obey the King's pleasure in all points and to leave 'such slanderous fashion as hath engendered unto him the displeasure of God and of his master'. Sir Henry then assured Cromwell that Thomas had mended his ways and that if he had not been entirely certain of this, he would refuse Thomas as his son.[2]

Thomas Wyatt's release from the Tower only weeks after the execution of Queen Anne and the men accused with her was probably due, in large part, to the intervention of Thomas Cromwell. That Cromwell should act on Wyatt's behalf is, perhaps, not so surprising, since he had close ties with the family. However, it is certain that Cromwell would not have been able to effect Wyatt's release had the King opposed it. Wyatt's escape from execution and his eventual freedom was ultimately due to Henry VIII and his belief in the poet's innocence. It certainly does seem that Thomas Wyatt owed his salvation to the fact that he, unlike those who had died with Anne, was known for certain to have had nothing to do with her since she became Henry's wife and queen. Wyatt, whatever relationship he had previously shared with Anne, was now firmly in the past.

Even Nicolas Sander was aware of this. According to him,[3] King Henry had told Anne everything that Thomas Wyatt had said about her in the council. As a result of this, Anne shunned Wyatt, and this distance between them had saved the poet's life. Had he maintained a close relationship with Anne, he might have been executed beside her other alleged lovers, 'when Anne's incest and adultery were detected'.

Wyatt's detachment from Anne was such that he did not directly connect his imprisonment with her fall. Rather, he attributed it to Charles Brandon, Duke of Suffolk, with whom he had already had serious altercations. It was Suffolk who, according to Sander,[4] had repeated Wyatt's opinion of Anne Boleyn's supposedly less than spotless reputation.

However, the Duke of Suffolk was King Henry's closest friend and, formerly, his brother-in-law. Suffolk had married Mary, the widow of King Louis XII of France, and she had died within a month of Anne's coronation. Years previously, when Mary was newly widowed, she had brazenly pursued and, if reading between the lines yields an accurate picture of the events, manipulated Suffolk into marrying her. This behaviour earned her the disapproval of Anne Boleyn and it is known that Anne and

Mary cordially disliked one another. It is possible that this dislike extended to Anne's friends and supporters for, whatever the initial cause of it, a degree of enmity certainly did exist between Charles of Suffolk and Thomas Wyatt. This had made itself felt in 1530, when Suffolk was briefly banished from court.

Moreover, when Wyatt was arrested for the final time in 1541, he referred to the events of May 1536, for which he held Suffolk responsible:

> My Lord of Suffolk himself can tell that I imputed it to him, and not only at the beginning but even the very night before my apprehension now last; what time I remember my saying unto him for his favour to remit his old undeserved evil will; and to remember 'like as he was a mortal man so to bear no immortal hate in his breast'. Although I had received the injury at his hands, let him say whether this be true.[5]

Wyatt's arrest at the time of Anne's fall is often considered to have been unconnected with it, or that it was done in order to lend verisimilitude to the proceedings. However, it now appears that there was some connection after all, and that it was related not only to Wyatt having 'known' Anne, but also his enmity with Suffolk which, in part at least, also had some connection with Anne.

Thomas Wyatt survived the events of May 1536. This might have come as some surprise to the poet. He notes that he had been warned by Stephan, an astrologer, that the month of May, during which love was celebrated so lavishly at the court of King Henry, would be unlucky for him:

Ye that in love find luck and sweet abundance,
And live in lust and joyful jollity,
Arise for shame, do away your sluggardy:
Arise, I say, do May some observance.
Let me in bed lie dreaming in mischance;
Let me remember my mishaps unhappy,
That me betide in May most commonly;
As one whom love list little to advance.
Stephan said true, that my nativity
Mischanced was with the ruler of May.
He guessed (I prove) of that the verity.
In May my wealth, and eke my wits, I say,
Have stond so oft in such perplexity:
Joy, let me dream of your felicity.[6]

Epilogue:
After Anne

Anne Boleyn was dead. Some of the men whose lives she touched, however fleetingly, followed her to the grave. For others, the world continued. Following the failure of the marriage negotiations that would have made Anne Boleyn his wife, James Butler[1] remained at the English court until February 1528. Leaving for Ireland, he took Keappahedin Castle as his seat and, in 1530, married Joan, daughter and heiress of James Fitzgerald, the late Earl of Desmond.

Butler, his father and brothers, became increasingly involved in disagreements with the Fitzgeralds of Kildare in Leinster. He raided the estates of Fitzgerald supporters and imposed coign and livery upon them. This was illegal but, rather than punishing him for it, King Henry rewarded Butler, making him lord treasurer of Ireland with a seat on the Irish council.

With Butler's agitation of the Fitzgeralds continuing, it was only a matter of time before full-scale hostilities ensued. This they did in September 1532. When attacked by forces led by the pro-Fitzgerald MacGillapatricks, Butler managed to escape with his life, although his brother, Thomas, was killed. Butler tracked down Thomas's killers, discovering them as they were being welcomed back to camp by the brother of the Earl of Kildare. Butler gave an account of the attack and the perpetrators to King Henry, who dealt with Kildare.

Upon the outbreak of the Kildare rebellion, in 1534, Butler earned further royal favour by subduing the rebel forces. Landmarks of his activities in this crisis are the defence of the town of Kilkenny, in August 1534, and the seizure of Dungarvan Castle, in October 1355. Butler was awarded the post of lord admiral of Ireland and warden of the ports in May 1535 by his grateful king. In autumn of that year, he was elevated to the dignity of Viscount Thurles.

With the fall of the Kildares, the Butlers of Ormond became the most powerful dynasty in Ireland. Fears on the part of the crown that they would replace the Kildares as a threat to English security proved to be unfounded. The Butlers had strong links with the English court. Moreover, James Butler apparently supported the reformation of the church, now being actively pursued by King Henry.

Still, tensions persisted. Butler faced a threat from Leonard Grey, the lord deputy of Ireland. There had long been conflict between the Greys and the Butlers. As it now happened, Grey was attempting to campaign independently of the Irish lords, seeking neither their advice nor their approval. Butler suggested that Grey was Kildare reborn, and he entered into a conspiracy, possibly in league with Sir Anthony St Leger, to oust Grey from office. In this endeavour, Butler had the support of other members of the Irish council, even those who had previously been critical of him. Grey was disgraced in 1540 and executed the following year.

Meanwhile, Piers Butler, James's father, died; James became ninth Earl of Ormond and second Earl of Ossory in August 1539. In July of the following year, Ormond's ally, Sir Anthony St Leger was appointed lord deputy of Ireland.

St Leger embarked upon a series of reforms with a view to introducing an English-style socio-economic structure to Gaelic Ireland. He began by urging Henry VIII to accept kingship of Ireland. St Leger could now claim to be working as a member of the King's party, which gave his reforms much more weight. One of his reforms involved the implementation of the policy of surrender and regrant. Under its terms, Gaelic chiefs were encouraged to surrender their lands to the crown, which would then regrant them in return for oaths of loyalty and a commitment to adopt English ways.

Throughout this, St Leger was supported by Ormond, who met the Gaelic chiefs in the Irish House of Lords and explained the new measures to them in Gaelic. Through St Leger, Ormond was acquainted with the new conservative faction that had emerged at the English court following the fall of Thomas Cromwell. Still, St Leger felt intimidated by Ormond's increasing power. As a counter-weight, he sought to promote the Earl of Desmond and other prominent Irish nobles into important positions in the royal administration. His advice on the matter was, however, not taken up by King Henry. A client of Ormond's, Walter Cowley, master of the rolls, launched an attack of St Leger, accusing him of corruption and, more immediately damaging, of seeking to revive the power of the Geraldines. Cowley found no support, his claims were rejected and he was dismissed from office.

Hostilities were temporarily set aside when Henry went to war with France. Ormond's willingness and ability to muster and supply troops for the King challenged St Leger's allegation that Ormond was ambitious and a danger to the crown. Relations worsened when the two men quarrelled, in 1544, about the raising of 2,000 kerne. Ormond was given joint command alongside Matthew Stewart, Earl of Lennox, for an invasion of western Scotland to subdue the regent, James Hamilton. Successful diplomacy led to the mission being aborted, nevertheless, Ormond's conduct served to consolidate his standing still further with King Henry.

Notwithstanding this, Ormond resented being given the command, interpreting it as a ploy to remove him from Ireland. He also accused St Leger of attempting to assassinate him. Mutual denunciations followed and the feud between the two men degenerated to the point that Henry felt obliged to step in.

Ormond and St Leger were summoned to court in April 1546. Their grievances were given due attention and, following an official investigation, St Leger was exonerated and returned to office. Ormond and seventeen of his followers were entertained at Limehouse, where they were served poisoned meat. Given recent events, St Leger has often been blamed for their deaths. However, he was almost certainly innocent. A contemporary chronicler stated that the meat had been poisoned by accident. Tellingly, as he lay dying, Ormond did not accuse St Leger, whom he made supervisor of his will. James Butler's life was tragically cut short at the age of about fifty; he was buried in the family vault, now disappeared, in the chapel of St Thomas the Martyr, Holborn. A tomb erected to his memory still exists in the choir of St Canice's Cathedral, Kilkenny. He left his wife, Joan, and their seven children, the eldest of whom, Thomas, became the tenth Earl of Ormond and third Earl of Ossory.

The life of Henry Percy, Earl of Northumberland after Anne was every bit as tragic as ever it had been.[2] The story of his failed marriage to Mary Talbot, unhappy as it was, found a forlorn parallel in the relations between Northumberland and his brothers, Sir Thomas and Sir Ingram.

Thomas and Ingram Percy were popular and active members of the wilder Marcher communities. It was here, in the untamed beauty of the Northumbrian countryside, that they learned the arts of confraternity and warfare under their uncle, Sir William, a veteran of Flodden. Thomas and Ingram had little time for their elder brother. Nevertheless, the earl was generous to his brothers, only to see them reward his kindness by joining forces with the supporters of the fallen William Lisle of Felton and other rebels.

As such, when Thomas asked to be made deputy warden of either the east or the middle March, Northumberland refused, giving the post to Lord Ogle instead. Thomas and Ingram were furious. They took their revenge by ordering their tenants not to respond to summonses from the deputy warden. Although Northumberland did give the post to his brother, Ingram, he withdrew it again shortly afterwards.

For their disloyalty and the depredations caused by the Percy brothers, Northumberland publicly threatened to disinherit them, instead leaving his patrimony to the crown. Having been given no reason to retract his words, Northumberland began a systematic break-up of his inheritance. Among the beneficiaries were friends and even former servants, such as Sir Reynold Carnaby, but the chief portion of the Northumberland estates would be granted to the crown. Nothing could dissuade the earl from this course. As he wrote to Cromwell, 'Perceiving the debility and unnaturalness of those of my name, I have determined to make the King my heir.'[3]

Northumberland especially ignored the rights of his wife. When the countess's father petitioned on her behalf he was told that, because he had not paid his daughter's dowry, the King would be under no obligation to pay her an allowance. This was to be the King's stance until the end of his life. It was only in 1549, under Henry's successor, Edward VI, that Countess Mary received a royal grant in compensation for her jointure.

The state of relations among the Percys had not mellowed at the opening of the Pilgrimage of Grace. While the Pilgrims were determined to have Northumberland's support, the earl was disinclined to grant it. Possibly, the principal reason for his reluctance was the enmity between himself and his brothers. His rapidly failing health was, however, another factor, for the earl was dying.

Still, following the Pilgrims' first assembly at Doncaster, their leader, Robert Aske, visited Northumberland at Wressell Castle. Aske, who was a former secretary to the earl as well as a distant relative by marriage, tried unsuccessfully to reconcile Northumberland with his brothers, both of whom had joined the rebellion. Another attempt was made to obtain the deputy wardenship of the Marches for Thomas and Ingram, but still the earl would not be moved.

Northumberland was visited next day by William Stapleton, a Pilgrim who might also have acted as an attorney on behalf of Northumberland. Stapleton found the earl in bed in a terrible state, 'weeping, ever wishing himself out of the world'. Aske then decided to press Northumberland, seeking to know whether he would at least support the action the Pilgrims were about to take. Northumberland replied that he would, although he continued to refuse to see his brother, Sir Thomas.

Northumberland was now in a dangerous situation because the commons, that is, the Pilgrims encamped outside the castle, were openly calling to 'strike off the head of the Earl and make Sir Thomas earl'. Another Pilgrim, Sir Thomas Hilton, when asked where Northumberland was, answered: 'he is now crept into a corner and dare not show himself, he hath made a many of knaves gentlemen to whom he had disposed much of his living and all now to do nought himself'.

Northumberland was now a prisoner within his own castle. With, perhaps, no other way out, he allowed himself to be sworn to the insurgents on 1 November. He asked the vicar of Baynton to send 'two gentlemen of worship to take him because he would be taken with no violence'. Wressell Castle was then given over to Aske, who made it his headquarters. Northumberland justified his action by saying he had wanted to escape from the commons and secure his evidences on the King's behalf. A very weak Northumberland was then taken to York, thence on to Selby.

On 3 June 1537, Northumberland made over his estates unconditionally to the crown. He asked only for some income to see him through what he was certain would be the last few weeks of his life. The earl was not exaggerating when he spoke of the rapid approach of his death. A description of the earl *in extremis* by the priest, Richard Layton, speaks of his sight and speech having failed him, 'his stomach swollen "so great as I never seen none", and his whole body as yellow as saffron, but his memory still good'.[4] Layton adds that for the last three weeks, that is, since he made over his estates to the crown, Northumberland had no money but by borrowing. King Henry, it seems, saw no reason to grant Northumberland's request to allow him a small income. It mattered little; within hours of Layton's visit, the sixth Earl of Northumberland was dead. He was buried in the Church of St Augustine, now St-John-at-Hackney.[5] His title lay in abeyance until 1557, when his nephew, Sir Thomas's son, also Thomas Percy, inherited it to become the seventh Earl of Northumberland.

As to Thomas Wyatt,[6] the bloody days of May 1536 had indeed changed him. His youthful good looks were replaced by the tired countenance of a man aged before his time. Still, as terrifying as his ordeal had been, he soon returned to favour upon his release from the Tower. As the Pilgrimage of Grace threatened, Wyatt was made steward of Conisborough Castle in Yorkshire, a post previously held by his father. Later in 1536, Wyatt was charged to raise 200 men to assist the Duke of Norfolk against the rebels. Unfortunately, the Pilgrims had been routed by the time he arrived.

Thomas Wyatt was then made Sheriff of Kent in 1536. The following year saw him in Spain, where he was to remain for two years. In his role as ambassador, Wyatt was to calm relations between Henry and Charles V. The Emperor was still indignant over the treatment of his aunt, the late Queen Katherine; he was also concerned to promote the claims of his cousin, Princess Mary. Wyatt's primary objective, though, was to prevent a *rapprochement* between Charles and François I. This was not easy to accomplish, since both men were impoverished by wars and were seeking peace. Wyatt's efforts were further hampered by the presence of Cardinal Pole, who had been sent to the Pope to unite Charles and François in league against Henry.

Wyatt sent his secretary, John Mason, to Pole to see what useful information could be gleaned from him. This action was deliberately misconstrued by Edmund Bonner, Archdeacon of Leicester and future 'Bloody Bonner', who had been sent to assist Wyatt. Bonner reported to Cromwell that Wyatt was holding treasonable correspondence with Pole, who was a sworn enemy of King Henry's, and of having treated the King with disrespect. Cromwell recognized in Bonner's words the contempt he had long held for Wyatt and Mason and so did not act. He filed the letter away and seems to have forgotten about it.

Wyatt next became involved in a plot to assassinate Cardinal Pole. On a visit home he discussed poison with his mistress, Elizabeth Darrell. He also mentioned the poison to King Henry, asking him if he should obtain some, Henry, however, dismissed the idea.

Wyatt completed his mission, without much success, and returned to Allington, where he spent the summer and autumn months renovating his home and attempting to put his confused and depleted finances in order. His happy domestic life, now shared openly with Elizabeth Darrell, was not to last; by mid-November, he was sent to continue his ambassadorial duties in the Low Countries.

Thomas Wyatt returned to Allington in May 1540 and, for once, the month proved kind to him. In June, however, storm clouds began to gather and Wyatt's protector and patron, Thomas Cromwell, was arrested. Wyatt might have witnessed the execution. Shortly afterwards, Bonner's incriminating letter was discovered and shown to the King. What Henry read led him to charge Wyatt with treason. Sir Richard Southwell was sent to Allington to arrest Wyatt, who was taken bound and handcuffed to the Tower. At his trial, Wyatt defended himself with spirit and wit, not forgetting the sarcasm he aimed at his accusers.

Wyatt's defence was a masterpiece of rhetoric, but his case still hung in the balance until Queen Katherine Howard interceded on the poet's behalf. Henry relented, but his conditions were harsh. Wyatt was to confess his guilt over the charges against him, he was leave his beloved mistress and return to his wife. Notwithstanding the irony of this last order, considering the past behaviour of the man who had issued it, Wyatt had little choice but to agree.

Freed from the Tower, Wyatt returned to Allington, where he wrote satires addressed to his friend, John Pointz, and composed his own version of the Seven Penitential Psalms. His rehabilitation was as rapid now as it had been in 1536. Wyatt was given the command of 300 horse in Calais. Grants of lands and offices culminated in his appointment as knight of the shire and MP for Kent. Among the dissolved monastic properties granted to him was the Carmelite priory in Aylesford, near Allington. Rumours that Wyatt was to become vice-admiral of the fleet circulated in August 1542, although nothing came of it.

Life now followed a quieter, if unhappy, course for Thomas Wyatt. Reunited with his wife, whom he had not seen for fifteen years or more, his thoughts were for Mistress Darrell alone. Frightened by his recent brush with death and alarmed by increasingly violent headaches, he made his will in June 1541. His heir was, of course, his son, Thomas. However, Wyatt provided for Elizabeth Darrell and their son, Francis.

As the autumn mists settled upon 1542, Wyatt was called upon to meet the envoys of Charles V, who were expected to land at Falmouth, and to escort them to London. As he hurried to the coast, Wyatt became overheated and his exertions led to a violent fever. He stopped at Sherborne, where his friend Sir John Horsey lived and, clearly unwell, he took to his bed. Three days later, Thomas Wyatt died, probably of pneumonia, at the age of thirty-nine. He rests in the Horsey family vault in Sherborne Abbey.

References

Abbreviations

CSP – Calendar of State Papers, Domestic Series, of the reign of Elizabeth I

CSP Foreign – Calendar of State Papers, Foreign Series, of the reign of Elizabeth I

CSP Spain – Calendar of Letters... and State Papers... between England and Spain, 1536–1538

CSP Venice – Calendar of State Papers Relating to English Affairs in the Archives of Venice

DNB – Oxford Dictionary of National Biography

LP – Letters and Papers, Foreign and Domestic, Henry VIII

Chapter 1. Growing up at Hever 1501–1513

  1. Frazer, p.115

  2. Ives, *Anne Boleyn*, pp.14-15

Chapter 2. The Coming of Grace: Anne & Margaret, Archduchess of Austria 1513–1514

  1. Bonnechose, p.221

2. Sergeant, *Anne Boleyn*, pp.12-13

3. Sergeant, *Anne Boleyn*, pp.17-18

4. Bridge, volume IV, p.231

5. *LP*, I.2375

6. De Iongh, pp.150-151

Chapter 3. The Rival of Venus: Anne in France 1514–1521

1. *LP*, I.3210

2. *LP*, I.3416

3. *LP*, I.3416

4. Sichel, p.92

5. *LP*, II.222

6. Strickland, *Lives*, volume I, p.165

7. Matarasso, p.248

8. cited in Strickland, *Lives*, volume I, pp.167-8

9. Strickland, *Lives*, volume I, p.167

Chapter 4. An Irish Alliance: Anne & James Butler 1521–1522

1. LaFayette, *The Princesse de Clèves*, p.60

2. *LP*, III.1994

3. Starkey, *Holbein's Irish Sitter*

4. Sander, *Schism*, p.25

5. Wyatt, 'Anne Boleigne', p.423-4

6. Sander, *Schism*, p.25

7. Sander, *Schism*, p.25

8. *CSP Venice, 1527–33*. 824

9. Sander, *Schism*, p.25

10. Wyatt, *Poetical Works*, p.6

11. Cavendish, *Life of Wolsey*, second ed., p.424

12. *CSP Venice, 1527–33.* 824

13. *CSP Venice, 1527–33.* 236

14. de Carles, p.3

15. *CSP Spain*, VI. 967

16. Sander, *Schism*, p.25

17. ibid

18. *LP*, VI. 585

19. Wyatt, 'Anne Boleigne', p.424

20. ibid

Chapter 5. An Innocent Love Affair: Anne & Henry Percy 1522–1524

1. Starkey, *Six Wives*, p.268

2. Jamison, *Talbot Papers*, p.339

3. Edwards, *DNB* online edition

4. Cavendish, *Life of Wolsey*, pp.57-58

5. Lancelott, *The Queens of England*, p.361

6. Ives, *Anne Boleyn*, pp.13-14

7. Brenen, *House of Percy*, vol I, p.152

8. Cavendish, *Life of Wolsey*, p.65

9. Burnet, *History of the Reformation*, volume 1, p.87

10. Strickland, *Lives*, vol I, p.178

11. Lancelott, *The Queens of England*, pp.363-4

Chapter 6. 'Where Force and Beauty Met': Anne & Thomas Wyatt
1524–1526

1. Bruce, 'Anecdotes', pp.236-7

2. Bruce, 'Anecdotes', p.237

3. *LP*, XVI.662

4. Howard, *Poems*, p.61

5. *Chronicle of King Henry VIII of England*, p.63

6. Wyatt, 'Anne Boleigne', p.424

7. Wyatt, 'Anne Boleigne', pp.424-5

8. Muir, *Life and Letters*, p.16

9. Gilfillan, *Poetical Works*, p.168

10. Arber, *Tottel's Miscellany*, pp.36-7

11. Harpsfield, *Treatise*, p.253

12. *LP*, X. 177, 999

13. Hoyle, 'Henry Percy', *The Tudor Nobility*, p.193

14. Martin, *DNB*

15. Sander, *Schism*, pp.28-30

16. Wyatt, 'Anne Boleigne', p.425

17. Gilfillan, *Poetical Works*, p.16

18. Bruce, 'Anecdotes', p.237

Chapter 7. Anne's Revenge 1527–1530

1. *CSP Spain, 1527–29.* 224

2. Ives, *Anne Boleyn*, p.65

3. Cavendish, *Life of Wolsey*, second edition, pp.468–469

4. Cavendish, *Life of Wolsey*, p.207

5. *LP*, IV.6030

6. Cavendish, *Life of Wolsey*, p.219

7. Cavendish, *Life of Wolsey*, pp.220-21

8. *LP*, IV.6199

Chapter 8. Henry Percy & the Arrest of Cardinal Wolsey 1530

1. *LP*, IV.3383

2. Cavendish, *Life of Wolsey*, pp.275-82

Chapter 9. The Pre-Contract 1532

1. Brenan, *House of Percy*, p.187

2. Cavendish, *Life of Wolsey*, second edition, p.463

3. *LP*, IV.3378

4. Brenan, *House of Percy*, p.203

5. Friedmann, *Anne Boleyn*, p.160

6. Brenan, *House of Percy*, p.223

7. *CSP Spain*, V. (i), p.33

Chapter 10. 'Some Tyme I Fled' 1532–1533

1. *CSP Spain*, IV (i), 302

2. Nicolas, *Poetical Works*, p.174

3. *LP*, VI.180

4. Friedmann, *Anne Boleyn*, p.190

5. *LP*, VI.701

6. *LP*, VI.1599

Chapter 11. All the Queen's Men: The Perils of Courtly Love, May 1536

1. *LP*, X.793

2. *LP*, IV.1906, 1907

3. *LP*, IV.4993

4. *LP*, X.793

5. *LP*, X.793

6. *CSP Foreign, Elizabeth I.*1303 (16-18)

7. Walker, 'Rethinking', p.5

8. *LP*, X.782

9. Sergeant, *Life of Anne Boleyn*, p.278

10. *LP*, X.798

11. Cavendish, 'Metrical Visions', pp.36-37

12. Amyot, 'A Memorial', p.64

13. *Chronicle of King Henry VIII of England*, p.61

14. de Carles, p.19

15. *LP*, X.798

16. Cavendish, 'Metrical Visions', p.30

17. *LP*, X.793

18. Davies, *DNB*, online edition

19. Ives, *DNB*, online edition

20. Hope, *DNB*, online edition

21. Ives, *DNB*, online edition

Chapter 12, 'Myn Extreme Enemye': Thomas Wyatt, May 1536

1. *LP*, VII. 922(17)

2. *Chronicle of King Henry VIII of England*, pp.63-64

3 Muir, *Life and Letters*, pp.29-30; *LP*, X.798

4. Bruce, 'Anecdotes', p.239

5. *LP*, X.819

6. *LP*, X.840

Chapter 13. *Circa Regna Tonat*, 12 May 1536

1. *LP*, X.848]

2. *LP*, X.855

3. *LP*, X.908

4. Wriothesley, 1.xxvii; *LP*, X.908

5. Walker, 'Rethinking', pp.8-9

6. Walker, 'Rethinking', pp.19-20

7. Ives, *Anne Boleyn*, p.336

8. Ives, *Anne Boleyn*, p.327

9. *LP*, V.907

10. *LP*, VI.733

11. *CSP Spain* V (i), 122

12. *LP*, VI.923

13. *LP*, VIII.862

14. *LP*, VI.613

15. *LP*, X.793

16. *LP*, X.855

17. *LP*, X.865

Chapter 14. Persecuted Innocence, 13–16 May 1536

1. Brenan, *House of Percy*, p.226

2. *CSP Spain* V (i), 122

3. *LP*, VIII.121

4. *CSP Spain*, V (ii), 47

5. *LP*, X.784

6. *LP*, X.782

7. Cavendish, *Life of Wolsey*, second edition, pp.464-5

8. Hoyle, 'Henry Percy', *The Tudor Nobility*, p.202

9. *LP*, X.908

10. *LP*, X.876

11. *LP*, X.876

12. *Chronicle of King Henry VIII of England*,
    volume 1, p.40-41

13. Ives, *Anne Boleyn*, p.422, note 68

14. *LP*, X.909

Chapter 15. 'The Bell Towre Showed me Suche a Syght', 17 May
    1536

1. *LP*, X.920

2. *LP*, X.1131

3. Sander, *Schism*, p.30

4. Sander, *Schism*, p.30

5. cited in Muir, *Life and Letters*, p.22

6. Gilfillan, *Poetical Works*, pp.4-5

Epilogue: After Anne

1. Edwards, *DNB*, online edition; Brysson, *DNB*, online edition

2. Hoyle, *DNB*, online edition; Brenan, *House of Percy*

3. *LP*, VIII.166

4. *LP*, XII.165

5. Walford, *Old and New London*, British History Online

6. Gilfillan, *Poetical Works*, pp.xii.xiv; Muir, *Life and Letters*; Burrow, *DNB*

Bibliography

Arber, E. (ed), *Tottel's Miscelleny: Songes and Sonettes written by the ryght honourable Lorde Henry Hawar late Earle of Surrey and other* (London: Apud Richardum Tottel. Cum priuilegio ad imprimendum solum, 1557). A collection of poems by Henry Howard, Earl of Surrey, Thomas Wyatt and others.

Amyot, T. (ed), 'A memorial from George Constantine', *Archaeologica*, 23 (1831). George Constantine was a servant to Henry Norris and went to school with William Brereton. His memorial contains reports concerning the fall of Anne Boleyn.

Bonnechose, Emile de, *History of France, from the Invasion of the Franks Under Clovis, to the Accession of Louis Philippe* (London: Routledge, 1856). A general history of France.

Brenan, George, *A History of the House of Percy* (London: Fremantle & Co, 1902). A history of the Percy family from its origins.

Bridge, John S.C., *A History of France from the Death of Louis XI* (Oxford: Clarendon Press, 1929). A general history of France.

Bruce, John, 'Unpublished Anecdotes of Sir Thomas Wyatt the Poet, and of other members of that family', *Gentleman's*

Magazine, volume 34, new series, (July to December, 1850). A collection of legends concerning the Wyatt family.

Brysson, Alan, 'St Leger, Sir Anthony (1496?–1559), *lord deputy of Ireland*', *Oxford Dictionary of National Biography*, Oxford University Press, 2004, online edition. A general biography.

Burnet, Gilbert, *The History of the Reformation of the Church of England* (Oxford: Clarendon Press, 1865). A huge work in several volumes laying out the history of the Reformation.

Burrow, Colin, 'Wyatt, Sir Thomas (*c*.1503–1542)', *Oxford Dictionary of National Biography*, Oxford University Press, 2004, online edition. A general biography.

Carles, Lancelot de, *Epistre contenant le Proces Criminel faite a l'encontre de la Royne Anne Boullant d'Angleterre* (Lyon, 1545). A contemporary poem relating the fall of Anne Boleyn.

Cavendish, George, *The Life of Cardinal Wolsey and Metrical Visions*, ed. S.W. Singer, volume 2 (Chiswick: Harding, Triphook, and Lepard, 1825). A two-volume biography of Cardinal Wolsey by his gentleman usher. Volume two contains biographies, in verse, of the main characters involved in the fall of Anne Boleyn and others, as well as contemporary letters.

Calendar of Letters... and State Papers... between England and Spain 1536–1538

Calendar of Letters... and State Papers... between England and Spain, Further Supplement 1513–1542

Calendar of the manuscripts of the most hon. the marquis of Salisbury, 1, HMC, 9 (1883)

Calendar of the Patent Rolls preserved in the Public Record Office... Henry VII

Calendar of State Papers, Domestic Series, of the reign of Elizabeth I

Calendar of State Papers, Foreign Series, of the reign of Elizabeth I

Calendar of State Papers Relating to English Affairs in the Archives of Venice: volume IV, 1527–1533 (1871)

Edwards, A.S.G., 'Cavendish, George (*b.*1494, *d.* in or before 1562?)', *Oxford Dictionary of National Biography*, Oxford University Press, 2004, online edition. A general biography.

Edwards, David, 'Butler [Bocach], James, ninth earl of Ormond and second earl of Ossory (*b.* in or after 1496, *d.*1546) nobleman', *Oxford Dictionary of National Biography* Oxford University Press, 2004, online edition. A general biography.

Fraser, Antonia, *The Six Wives of Henry VIII*, (London: Weidenfeld and Nicholson, 1992). A study of the six wives for the general reader.

Friedmann, P., *Anne Boleyn: a Chapter of English History, 1527–1536* (London:, Macmillan and Co, 1884). A two-volume early biography of Anne Boleyn, very detailed.

Gilfillan, George (ed), *The Poetical Works of Sir Thomas Wyatt* (Edinburgh: James Nichol; London: James Nisbet; Dublin: W. Robertson, 1858). A collection of Wyatt's poems; also contains a biography and a transcript of his defence.

Harpsfield, Nicholas, *A Treatise on the Pretended Divorce between Henry VIII and Catherine of Aragon*, ed. N. Pocock Camden Society, 2nd series 21 (1878). Primarily an attack on

Cranmer and a refutation of the canon law case for Henry VIII's divorce from Queen Katherine; very disparaging towards Anne Boleyn.

Hope, Andrew, 'Constantine, George (*b. c.*1500, *d.* in or before 1561)', *Oxford Dictionary of National Biography*, Oxford University Press, 2004, online edition. A general biography.

Howard, Henry, *The Poems of Henry Howard, Earl of Surrey* (London: William Pickering, 1831). A collection of poems by Henry Howard, Earl of Surrey as well as a memoir of the poet.

Hoyle, R.W., 'Percy, Henry Algernon, sixth earl of Northumberland, (*c.*1502–1537), *magnate*, *Oxford Dictionary of National Biography*, Oxford University Press, 2004, online edition. A general biography.

Hoyle, R.W., 'Henry Percy, sixth earl of Northumberland and the Fall of the House of Percy, 1527–1537' in G.W. Bernard (ed.) *The Tudor Nobility* (Manchester: Manchester University Press, 1992). A study of the break-up of the Percy estates; contains some biographical material.

Hume, M.A.S., *Chronicle of King Henry VIII of England* (London: Bell, 1889). A translation of a Spanish chronicle; contemporary with the events it describes.

Iongh, Jane De, *Margaret of Austria: regent of the Netherlands*; trans. by M.D. Herter Norton (London: Cape, 1954). A biography of the Archduchess.

Ives, Eric, *The Life and Death of Anne Boleyn: 'the most happy'* (Oxford: Blackwell Publishing Ltd, 2004). A detailed, scholarly biography of Anne Boleyn.

Ives, E.W., 'Brereton, William (*c*.1487x90–1536)', *Oxford Dictionary of National Biography*, Oxford University Press, September 2004, online edition. A general biography.

Jamison, Catherine (ed), *A Calendar of the Shrewsbury and Talbot papers in Lambeth Palace Library and the College of Arms* (London, HMSO, 1966). A transcript of the papers belonging to the Talbot family.

LaFayette, Madame de, *The Princess of Clèves* (Oxford: University Press, 1999). A seventeenth-century novel.

Lancelott, Francis, *The Queens of England and their Times* (New York: D. Appleton and Company, 1858). A history of the Queens of England from Matilda of Flanders to Adelaide of Saxe-Meinengen.

Letters and Papers, Foreign and Domestic, Henry VIII

Martin, C. T., 'Bonvisi, Antonio (1470x75–1558)', rev. Basil Morgan, *Oxford Dictionary of National Biography*, online edition. A general biography.

Matarasso, Pauline, *Queen's Mate. Three Women of Power in France on the eve of the Renaissance* (Aldershot: Ashgate, 2001). A biographical study of Anne of France, Anne of Brittany and Louise of Savoy.

Muir, Kenneth, *Life and Letters of Sir Thomas Wyatt* (Liverpool: Liverpool University Press, 1963). A biography of the poet, with letters and poems as source material.

Nicolas, Nicholas Harris, *The Poetical Works of Sir Thomas Wyatt* (London, W. Pickering, 1831). A collection of poems with biography and a transcript of Wyatt's defence.

Sander, Nicolas, *The Rise and Growth of the Anglican Schism* (London: Burns & Oates, 1877). A study of Henry VIII's divorce and the Reformation from a Catholic perspective.

Sergeant, Philip W., *The Life of Anne Boleyn* (New York: D. Appleton and Company, 1924). An early study of Anne Boleyn.

Sichel, Edith, *Women and Men of the French Renaissance* (Westminster: Archibald Constable & Co, Ltd; Philadelphia: J.B. Lippincott Company, 1901). A study of the French Renaissance with emphasis on Margaret of Angoulême and François Rabelais.

Starkey, David, 'Holbein's Irish Sitter', *The Burlington Magazine*, Vol. 123, No. 938 (May, 1981). Identifies the portrait formerly thought to be that of Thomas Boleyn as that of James Butler.

Starkey, David, *Six Wives: The Queen's of Henry VIII* (London: Vantage, 2004). A detailed and scholarly study of Henry VIII's six wives focusing primarily on Katherine of Aragon and Anne Boleyn.

Strickland, Agnes, *Lives of the Queens of England* second edition (Philadelphia: Lea & Blanchard, 1842). A multi-volume biographical study of the Queens of England.

Walford, Edward, Walford, *Old and New London*, volume 5, British History Online. A history of London.

Walker, Greg, 'Rethinking the fall of Anne Boleyn', *The Historical Journal*, Vol. 45, No.1 (March 2002), pp.1-29. Revises the evidence for the fall of Anne Boleyn, concludes that Anne was condemned not for what she did, but for what she said.

Wriothesley, Charles, *A Chronicle of England, 1485-1559*, ed. W.D Hamilton. Camden Society, 2nd series, 11 & 20 (1875, 1877). A chronicle of England by a contemporary herald.

Wyatt, George, 'The Life of Queen Anne Boleigne' in *The Life of Cardinal Wolsey by George Cavendish*, second edition, ed. S.W. Singer (London: Harding and Lepard, Pall Mall East, 1827). A sympathetic biography of Anne Boleyn by the grandson of the poet, Thomas Wyatt.

Wyatt, Thomas, *The Poetical Works of Thomas Wyatt* (London: William Pickering, 1831). A collection of the poet's works, as well as biographical details and a transcript of Wyatt's defence.

List of Illustrations

1. Allington Castle, Kent. The home of Thomas Wyatt. © Josephine Wilkinson.
2. Alnwick Castle, Northumberland. Henry Percy's primary residence as Earl of Northumberland. © Josephine Wilkinson.
3. Anne Boleyn from the portrait held at Hever Castle. The rival of Venus. © Hever Castle Ltd.
4. Anne Boleyn from the portrait held at Ripon Cathedral and recently heralded as likely to be closest depiction of Anne. By kind permission of the Chapter of Ripon Cathedral.
5. Autograph of Henry Percy, sixth Earl of Northumberland. © Josephine Wilkinson.
6. Anne Boleyn from the portrait held in the Royal Collection. © Jonathan Reeve JR995b66fp24 15001600.
7. Anne Boleyn as depicted in historical fiction. © Jonathan Reeve JR1148b68fp3 15001600.
8. Anne by Hans Holbein. © Elizabeth Norton and the Amberley Archive.
9. Typical dress of a Tudor lady in waiting by Hans Holbein. © Elizabeth Norton and the Amberley Archive.

28. James Butler. © Jonathan Reeve JR974b61p686 15001600.

29. Thomas Wyatt. © Elizabeth Norton and the Amberley Archive.

30. Thomas Cromwell. © Josephine Wilkinson.

31. Cardinal Thomas Wolsey. © Josephine Wilkinson.

Index